The Art of

Phonics

Jenny Pearson

The Art of Phonics

Jenny Pearson

Copyright © 2018 Kivett Publishing

Kivett Publishing

ISBN: 978-1-941691-41-0

Language Arts > Phonics

TABLE OF CONTENTS

INTRODUCTION

What makes phonics difficult to learn?

- Similar letter patterns can make different sounds.

  tough / though / through / thought

- There are multiple ways to make the same sound.

  rain / play / they / make / eight / break

- Technical jargon sometimes adds confusion.

We avoided technical jargon to help make the concepts clear. (For those who wish to learn the technical terms, these are collected in the Appendix.)

- Students need practice that helps build confidence.

Use the key at the back of the book to check your work.

- It helps to feel comfortable with the resources.

We attempted to make this book appeal to all ages. Teens and adults may appreciate the lack of pictures, and some kids appreciate this, too.

TIPS

Remember to check your answers to the exercises with the answers tabulated at the back of this book.

As you read this book, speak the words out loud. This will give you valuable practice.

In the summer of 2018, this book will also become available as an audio book. This will help you listen to the proper pronunciation as you read the words.

Listen to spoken English in audio books and videos, as this will help you remember how many words sound.

Participate in conversations in English, as this will help to develop your communication skills.

VOWEL SOUNDS

(A Brief Intro)

- the long **a** sound:

  make (a_e) / play (ay) / they (ey) / rain (ai)

  angel (a) / eight (ei) / break (ea) / ballet (et)

- the long **e** sound:

  see (ee) / team (ea) / key (ey) / these (e_e)

  brief (ie) / ceiling (ei) / happy (y) / me (e)

- the long **i** sound:

  ice (i_e) / night (igh) / pie (ie) / try (y) / mind (i)

- the long **o** sound:

  no (o) / boat (oa) / phone (o_e) / grow (ow)

  toe (oe) / though (ough) / ou (shoulder)

- the long **u** sound:

  new (ew) / moon (oo) / tune (u_e) / through (ou)

true (ue) / flu (u) / fruit (ui) / soup (ou) / do (o)

- the short **a** sound:

  cat (a) / laugh (au) / plaid (ai)

- the short **e** sound:

  bed (e) / ready (ea) / friend (ie) / said (ai)

  says (ay) / any (a) / leopard (eo) / bury (u)

- the short **i** sound:

  is (i) / gym (y) / build (ui)

  women (e) / women (o) / business (u)

- the short **o** sound:

  hot (o) / father (a)

- the short **u** sound:

  cup (u) / ton (o) / blood (oo)

  trouble (ou)

- the **aw** sound:

  saw (aw) / cause (au) / taught (augh)

long (o) / talk (al) / bought (ough)

- the (short) **oo** sound:

book (oo) / could (ou) / push (u) / wolf (o)

- the **y +** long **u** sound:

use (u_e) / few (ew) / view (iew)

value (ue) / coupon (ou) / beauty (eau)

- the **y + oo** sound:

cure (u_e) / furious (u_i) / fury (u_y)

- the **oi** sound:

oil (oi) / boy (y) / buoyant (uoy)

- the **ow** sound:

cow (ow) / out (ou) / drought (ough)

- the soft **uh** sound:

a (a) / the (e) / ago (a)

item (e) / cousin (i) / carrot (o) / circus (u)

vinyl (y) / nation (io) / bargain (ai) / famous (ou)

- the 'l sound, which involves a much reduced **uh** sound coming after a **t** or a **d** (but not after **nd**):

  title (le) / vital (al)

- the 'n sound, which involves a much reduced **uh** sound coming after a **t** or a **d** (but not after **st** where **t** is silent):

  kitten (en) / carton (on)

- the **ir** sound:

  her (er) / sir (ir) / word (or) / turn (ur)

  pearl (ear) / syrup (yr) / nourish (our)

- the **w +** short **u** sound:

  one (o)

- the **w +** long **i** sound:

  choir (oi)

- vowel **+ r** sounds:

short **e + r**: care / chair / their / there / bear

short **o + r**: car / farm / heart / sergeant

o + r: more / for / four / war / door / roar

Note: You probably hear **more** and the other words above with the long **o** sound. (For technical reasons, they are classified as **aw + r,** but if you try to say **aw** when you say these words, it won't come out right.) Try to say long **o + r** when pronouncing the words above.

the **ir** sound: her / sir / word / turn / pearl

short **i + r**: ear / near / here / cheer / pier

uh + r : over / doctor / collar

long **i + r**: fire

oo + r: poor / tour

y + oo + r: cure

ow + r: sour

CONSONANT SOUNDS

(A Brief Intro)

- the **b** sound:

    big (b) / rabbit (bb)

- the **ch** sound:

    chin (ch) / watch (tch) / future (tu)

    question (ti) / righteous (te)

- the **d** sound:

 dog (d) / ladder (dd) / could (ld) / spelled (ed)

- the **f** sound:

    fun (f) / offer (ff) / phone (ph)

    rough (gh) / half (lf) / often (ft)

- the **g** sound:

    good (g) / egg (gg) / ghost (gh)

    guy (gu) / vague (gue)

- the **h** sound:

hat (h) / who (wh)

- the **j** sound:

    jet (j) / page (ge) / giant (gi) / gym (gy)

    edge (dg) / soldier (di) / gradual (du)

- the **k** sound:

    kid (k) / cat (c) / back (ck) / school (ch)

    soccer (cc) / talk (lk) / unique (qu) / box (x)

- the **l** sound:

    like (l) / tall (ll) / able (le)

    castle (tle) / island (sl)

- the **m** sound:

    mom (m) / summer (mm) / thumb (mb)

    calm (lm) / autumn (mn)

- the **n** sound:

    nap (n) / funny (nn) / knee (kn)

    gnat (gn) / pneumonia (pn)

- the **ng** sound (no clear **g** sound is heard, yet the **ng** sound is different from the **n** sound, as we will learn in Part 1):

ring (ng) / tongue (ngue) / pink (nk)

Note: **pink** ends with the **ng + k** sounds.

- the **p** sound:

pet (p) / happy (pp)

- the **r** sound:

run (r) / carry (rr) / write (wr) / rhyme (rh)

- the **s** sound:

sun (s) / toss (ss) / ice (c)

scent (sc) / psychology (ps) / castle (st)

- the **sh** sound:

shy (sh) / tension (si) / sure (su) / special (ci)

ocean (ce) / chef (ch) / motion (ti)

- the **t** sound:

    toy (t) / little (tt) / hoped (ed)

- the **th** sounds (two different kinds):

    the (*th*) / thing (th)

- the **v** sound:

    vine (v) / gave (ve) / of (f)

- the **w** sound:

    win (w) / why (wh) / penguin (u) / one (o)

- the consonant **y** sound:

    yes (y) / unique (u) / onion (i)

- the **z** sound:

    zoo (z) / buzz (zz) / was (s)

    scissors (ss) / xylophone (x)

- the **zh** sound:

    usual (s) / azure (z) / television (si)

    equation (ti) / beige (ge) / luxury (x)

PART 1

PRONOUNCING

CONSONANTS

CONSONANTS

Here we will group consonants together that make similar sounds. Practice saying each word. Try to hear the difference between similar sounds.

- Compare **b** (as in **bee**), **d** (as in **dog**), **p** (as in **pet**), and **t** (as in **to**).

  Compare **big, dig, pig** / **Compare rib, rid, rip**

  Compare bug, dug, tug / **Compare rob, rod, rot**

  Compare dip, tip / **Compare pad, pat**

- Compare **f** (as in **fish**), **v** (as in **very**), and **w** (as in **win**).

  Compare fan, van / **Compare safe, save**

  Compare vest, west / **Compare stove, stow**

- Compare **l** (as in **let**) and **r** (as in **red**).

  Compare lip, rip / **Compare scale, scare**

- Compare **m** (as in **me**) and **n** (as in **no**).

  Compare met, net / Compare came, cane

- Compare **h** (as in **hat**) and **y** (as in **yes**).

  Compare hello, yellow

- Compare **c** (as in **cat**), **g** (as in **go**), **j** (as in **jet**), **k** (as in **kid**), **q** (as in **queen**), **s** (as in **see**), **x** (as in **fix**), and **z** (as in **zero**).

  Compare cat, sat / Compare king, sing

  Compare sip, zip / Compare fussy, fuzzy

  Compare box, boss / Compare tack, tax

  Compare coat, quote / Compare get, jet

Note that **c, g, q, s,** and **x** can also make other sounds:

  ice (c like s) / age (g like j) / unique (q like k)

  rose (s like z) / xylophone (x like z)

SINGLE OR DOUBLE S

When the letter **s** begins a word or appears as a double

ss, it often sounds like the **s**'s in the word **class.**

see / mess / sit / likes / same

One **s** at the end of a plural or verb often sounds like **z.**

days / games / is / runs / has

An **s** between two vowel sounds may also sound like **z.**

visit / losing / risen

Note: The **s** in **house** doesn't appear between two vowel

sounds since the **e** is silent. Compare **house** to **housing.**

---

1. Circle the words where **s** sounds like **z.**

dogs / soft / was / kiss / music

2. Circle the words where **s** doesn't sound like **z.**

grass / easy / bees / space / cousin

S EXCEPTIONS

There are many exceptions to when an **s** sounds like a **z**.

- The **s**'s in **lose** and **hose** sound like **z**, yet the **e** is silent (it doesn't make a vowel sound). Compare with **loose** and **moose**, which don't sound like **z**.

- The **s**'s in **basic** and **beside** don't sound like **z**, even though the **s**'s appear between two vowel sounds.

- The **s**'s in **picnics** and **dots** don't sound like **z**, yet they are plurals.

- The double **ss** in **scissors** sounds like **z**.

- The word **close** can mean two different things: With an **s** sound, **close** means **near**. With a **z** sound, **close** means **shut**.

- The **s**'s in **desert** and **dessert** both sound like **z**. (The difference is how you pronounce the first **e**.)

SH, SU, AND SI

The letters **sh** make a special sound.

ship / share / wish / shoe / push

The letter **s** in **su** or **si** usually makes the **s** or **z** sound that we discussed on page 18. However, the letter pairs **su** and **si** occasionally sound like **sh**.

- In the following **su** and **si** examples, **s** sounds like **s**.

sun / super / missing / silent

- In the following **su** and **si** examples, **s** sounds like **z**.

raisin / resume / rising / visit

- In the following examples, **su** and **si** sound like **sh**.

sure / sugar / mission / passion

Note that **su** and **si** sometimes make a different sound.

In the following examples, **su** and **si** sound more like **zh**.

treasure / television / measure

MORE S NOTES

- The **s** in **this** doesn't sound like **z** because the word **this** is neither plural nor a verb. Compare with the plural **toys** and verb **runs**, where **s** sounds like **z**.

- The **s** in **always** sounds like a **z**, even though it is neither plural nor a verb.

- An **s** can be silent, like it is in the word **island**.

- Most other types of **s**'s (those we haven't discussed) sound like the **s**'s in the word **class**. The following words don't begin or end with **s**, don't have a single **s** between two vowel sounds, and aren't special letter pairs (like **sh**, **su**, or **si**).

    fast / risk / trust / basket / dense

There are a few exceptions, like those below.

    husband (z sound) / transmit (z sound)

1. In the word **doors,** the **s** sounds like ___.

s / z / sh / zh

2. In the word **star,** the **s** sounds like ___.

s / z / sh / zh

3. In the word **music,** the **s** sounds like ___.

s / z / sh / zh

4. In the word **sugar,** the **s** sounds like ___.

s / z / sh / zh

5. In the word **miss,** the **s's** sound like ___.

s / z / sh / zh

6. In the word **treasure,** the **s** sounds like ___.

s / z / sh / zh

7. In the word **mister,** the **s** sounds like ___.

s / z / sh / zh

8. In the word **husband,** the **s** sounds like ___.

s / z / sh / zh

HARD/SOFT C

Most of the time, the letter **c** sounds hard like **k**.

cat / color / cup / scare / back

When **c** is followed by **e, i,** or **y,** it is usually soft like **s**.

ice / cent / princess / city / bicycle

There is one common exception. In the word below, the second **c** is followed by an **e,** yet the **cc**'s sound like **k**.

soccer

---

1. Circle the words where **c** sounds hard like **k**.

cake / race / cute / scar / mice

2. Circle the words where **c** sounds soft like **s**.

cook / nice / close / icy / cities

3. In each word, circle the **c** that sounds soft like **s**.

circle / accept / bicycle / concert

CH, CE, AND CI

The letters **ch** make a special sound.

chair / lunch / inch / cheap / rich

The letters **tch** make a similar sound.

watch / catch / pitch / fetch / itch

There are a few exceptions, where **ch** sounds like **sh**.

chef / parachute

Rarely, **ch** can sound like **k** instead.

school / stomach / ache

The letters **ce** and **ci** occasionally make a **sh** sound.

ocean / special

---

1. Circle the words that make a **ch** sound.

lunch / dish / back / choose / especially

2. Circle the words that make a **ch** sound.

color / chain / pinch / clear / school

HARD/SOFT G

When **g** is followed by **a, o,** or **u,** it is usually hard.

game / go / garden / good / gum

When **g** is followed by **e, i,** or **y,** it is usually soft like **j.**

gentle / huge / giant / giraffe / allergy

Rarely, a soft **g** can sound more like **zh** than like **j.** Note the second **g** in the first example below.

garage / beige / massage

When **g** comes at the end of a word, it is usually hard.

bag / leg / dig / log / bug

When **g** is followed by a consonant other than **h** it is usually hard. (We will discuss **gh** on page 27.)

glad / grin / legs / gray / jingle

A double **gg** is also usually hard.

egg / bigger / hugging / jagged / digging

G EXCEPTIONS

- Here are some exceptions with a hard **g**.

  get / gear / gift / girl / tiger / target

- In the examples below, the first word has a hard g, whereas the second word has a soft g.

  anger / danger

- In the pairs **ng** and **gg**, it's common for a hard **g** to come before an **e** or an **i**.

  anger / finger / hunger / bigger / digging

- Here is an exception with a soft **g**.

  margarine

- Rarely, **gu** makes a **gw** sound, like the word **language** (the second **g** also makes the **j** sound).

- The **g** is silent in the word **sign**.

- We will consider the letters **gh** on the next page.

GH

The letters **gh** sometimes sound like **f**.

laugh / rough / tough / cough / enough

The letters **gh** are sometimes silent.

right / night / height / weigh / neighbor

Rarely, the **g** in **gh** can be hard, with **h** silent.

ghost

The words below have very similar spelling, yet **gh** sounds like **f** in the first word and is silent in the second, third, and fourth words.

tough / though / thought / through

You may also notice that the vowels **ou** sound differently in all of the words above. We will learn about vowel sounds in Part 2 of this book.

1. Circle the words where **g** sounds hard like **g**.

    large / galaxy / goat / engine / gut

2. Circle the words where **g** sounds soft like **j**.

    get / danger / region / apology / guitar

3. Circle the words that make an **f** sound.

    light / cough / tough / thought / weight

4. Circle the words where **gh** is silent.

    sight / rough / fight / through / laughter

5. In the word **great**, the **g** sounds like ___.

    g / j / zh / f

6. In the word **giant**, the **g** sounds like ___.

    g / j / zh / f

7. In the word **get**, the **g** sounds like ___.

    g / j / zh / f

8. In the word **tough**, the **g** sounds like ___.

    g / j / zh / f

DG AND NG

The letters **dg** usually make the **j** sound.

edge / ridge / badger / bridge / judging

The letters **ng** make a special sound. When the **g** begins a new syllable, it usually makes a clear hard **g** sound.

anger / longer / finger / jungle / hungry

However, when **ng** ends a word (like –ing verbs), there usually isn't a clear hard **g** sound at the end of the **ng.** Yet the **ng** sound is different from an ordinary **n.**

ring / being / strong / going / moving

A few exceptions to these rules include:

change and **danger** (where the **g** is soft)

language (where **gu** sounds like **gw**)

Rarely, the letter **d** sounds like **j** even when it doesn't come with a **g** (like **dg**). This mainly happens with **du.**

educate / graduate / individual / soldier

1. Circle the words that include a **j** sound.

badge / angry / bridges / fudge / changing

2. Circle the words that include a **j** sound.

grade / danger / finger / soldiers / education

3. Circle the words where a clear **g** sound follows **ng**.

bring / hunger / string / strongest / seeing

4. Circle the words no clear **g** sound follows **ng**.

fang / finger / sung / anger / doing

5. In the word **stronger**, the **g** sounds like ___.

g / gw / j / zh / f

6. In the word **stranger**, the **g** sounds like ___.

g / gw / j / zh / f

7. In the word **jingle**, is there a clear **g** sound?

yes / no

8. In the word **crying**, does **ng** make a clear **g** sound?

yes / no

T AND TH

When **t** isn't followed by an **h,** it makes the **t** sound.

at / team / sit / top / state

The letters **th** make two different special sounds. Note how the **th** sounds different in the first list below compared to the second list below.

the / that / father / this / there

thing / bath / teeth / with / thick

How do you know whether **th** will sound like the **th** in the word **that** or the **th** in the word **thing?** There are a few guidelines, which we will learn, but there are also exceptions. For the **th** words that are used frequently in the English language – like **the, that, there, this,** and **thing** – it helps if you can remember them. For less frequent **th** words, the guidelines will help, but remember that they aren't foolproof.

TH GUIDELINES

If a syllable ends with **th,** it is often **th** like **thing.**

with / both / breath / bath / without

If a word ends with **the,** it is often **th** like **that.**

breathe / bathe / clothe

If a word begins with **th** followed by a long **e** sound (like **see**) or a long **i** sound (like **kite**), it is often **th** like **thing.** One common exception is the word **these.**

thief / thigh / theme / theater / theory

If a word begins with **th** followed by a vowel sound that is different from a long **e** or **i,** it is often **th** like **that.**

the / that / them / this / there / thus / they

Following are common exceptions to the previous rule.

thin / think / thank / thick / thought / theft

The letters **thr** always use **th** like **thing.**

throw / three / thread / through / throat

1. In the word **cloth,** the **th** sounds like ___.

that / thing

2. In the word **clothe,** the **th** sounds like ___.

that / thing

3. In the word **thieves,** the **th** sounds like ___.

that / thing

4. In the word **than,** the **th** sounds like ___.

that / thing

5. In the word **though,** the first **th** sounds like ___.

that / thing

6. In the word **thumb,** the **th** sounds like ___.

that / thing

7. In the word **thrill,** the **th** sounds like ___.

that / thing

8. In the word **thankful,** the **th** sounds like ___.

that / thing

TI AND TU

The letters **ti** make the **sh** sound in the suffix **–tion** and many other suffixes where **ti** is followed by a vowel.

action / national / cautious / partial / patient

Otherwise, the **t** in **ti** makes the usual **t** sound.

tiger / entire / until / tiara / native

The letters **te**, **ti**, and **tu** sometimes make the **ch** sound.

actual / fortune / culture / question / righteous

Usually, **te**, **ti**, and **tu** make the normal **t** sound.

time / tune / nineteen / costume / turkey

Rarely, there can be two accepted pronunciations of the letter **t** in **tu**. One example is the word **congratulate**, where the first **t** may be pronounced as **ch** or **j**. (Normally, there is just one correct way pronounce a word.)

–ED PAST TENSE

The **d** and **t** sounds are distinctly different, with one exception: If a verb ends with a **ch, f, k, p, s, sh,** or **x** sound, the past tense form with **–ed** usually makes a **t** sound (without adding an extra syllable).

rea**ch**ed / lau**gh**ed (f sound) / coo**k**ed / tra**pp**ed

jui**c**ed (s sound) / fi**sh**ed / fi**x**ed

Otherwise, the past tense form with **–ed** usually makes a **d** sound. If a verb ends with a **t** or **d** sound (like **part**ed), add the syllable **id.** Otherwise, don't add a syllable.

peeled / named / moved / cared / used (z sound)

graded / **add**ed / **vot**ed / **start**ed / **dent**ed

There are a few exceptions to these rules. For example, **crooked** (2 syllables) ends with the **id** sound, while **cooked** (1 syllable) ends with a **t** sound.

1. Circle the words that include a **sh** sound.

   lotion / tiara / fortune / nutrition / ambitious

2. Circle the words that include a **ch** sound.

   tube / ritual / century / tuition / lecture

3. Circle the words that include a **t** sound.

   liked / needed / saved / pinched / washed

4. Circle the words that include a **d** sound.

   raced / rained / hired / seated / relaxed

5. In the word **cheated**, the **ed** sounds like ___ .

   t / d / id

6. In the word **looked**, the **ed** sounds like ___ .

   t / d / id

7. In the word **needed**, the **ed** sounds like ___ .

   t / d / id

8. In the word **changed**, the **ed** sounds like ___ .

   t / d / id

R AND W BLENDS

First consider the single **r** and **w** sounds.

red / far / rare / more / scary

water / wait / wing / wish / woman

The **dr** and **tr** blends make special sounds.

dry / dream / draw / try / trail / true

The **w** is silent in **wr**. This pair makes an **r** sound.

wrong / wrist / write / wrap / wrestle

The letters **wh** usually make a **w** sound. Exceptions include **who** and **whole,** where **wh** makes the **h** sound.

what / when / where / why / white

Other **r** and **w** blends tend to come more naturally.

broom / cry / free / green / proof

swing / sweet / between / twelve / twinkle

The **w** can also be part of a vowel sound. See Part 2.

1. In the word **war,** the **r** sounds like ___.

r / w / h

2. In the word **war,** the **w** sounds like ___.

r / w / h

3. In the word **wrote,** the **wr** sounds like ___.

r / w / h

4. In the word **while,** the **wh** sounds like ___.

r / w / h

5. In the word **rush,** the **r** sounds like ___.

r / w / h

6. In the word **watch,** the **w** sounds like ___.

r / w / h

7. In the word **wrench,** the **wr** sounds like ___.

r / w / h

8. In the word **who,** the **wh** sounds like ___.

r / w / h

PH AND QU

The letters **ph** usually make the **f** sound.

elephant / phonics / alphabet / telephone

The rare exceptions tend to be compound words.

uphill / uphold / loophole

The letters **qu** usually sound like **kw**.

quick / queen / quiet / require / liquid

When a word ends with **que**, it makes the **k** sound.

unique / antique / technique / picturesque

Here are two exceptions to when **qu** makes a **k** sound.

mosquito / turquoise

---

1. Circle the words that make the **f** sound.

phone / graph / rough / touch / uphill

2. Circle the words that make the **kw** sound.

quit / request / unique / question / mosquitoes

THE LETTER K

The letter **k** usually makes its normal **k** sound. The letters **ck** always make a **k** sound.

keep / kind / book / back / rock / check / lucky

The **k** is silent in words that begin with **kn.**

know / knee / knock / knight / knuckle

When we blend the **n** and **k** sounds together to form **nk,** the **n** sounds similar to how it sounds in many **ng** words. It may help to review page 29. For example, compare how the **n** sounds in the words **sink** and **sing.**

bank / pink / skunk / ankle / monkey

Other **k** blends tend to come more naturally.

skip / work / milk / ask / books

---

1. Circle the words where **k** is silent.

knit / stink / kiss / knot / wrinkle

40

THE LETTER L

You may notice a slight difference in the way that the lowercase letter l sounds depending on whether it comes before or after a vowel sound.

like / lamp / lean / long / lose

cool / tall / rule / fill / owl

You may also notice that l seems to blend a little differently with other letters depending on whether it comes before or after another consonant.

blue / clean / flat / glue / play / slide

hold / elf / wolf / else / melt / elbow

Compare how l sounds at the end of these words:

able / title / handle / little / sprinkle

The l sound is also common in many adverbs.

nicely / fully / slowly / carefully / wildly

The l can even be silent, as in **talk** or **would**.

X AND Z

The letter **z** usually makes its normal **z** sound.

zoo / zero / prize / cozy / amazing

Rarely, the **z** sounds like **zh**. A **z** can even sound like a **t** or an **s** (like the last two examples below).

azure (zh) / seizure (zh) / pizza (ts) / pretzel (ts)

The letter **x** often sounds like **ks**.

box / taxi / except / complex / maximum

When **x** begins a word, it usually sounds like **z**.

xerox / xylophone

The letter **x** can also make the **gz** sound.

exam / exact / example / exist / anxiety

The word **luxury** can be pronounced with **ksh** or **gzh**.

Note that **anxiety** is pronounced with **gz**, but **anxious** is pronounced with **ksh**.

Y, U, I, and O

The consonant **y** usually sounds like a consonant when it begins a syllable. (Part 2 covers vowel sounds.)

yes / you / yellow / beyond / yo-yo

The vowel **u** sometimes makes the **yu** sound. (Part 2 covers vowel sounds.)

use / unique / usual / cute / future

However, the letter **u** doesn't always sound like a consonant at the beginning of a word.

under / unlike / ugly / urn / up

In the word **unusual**, the first **u** sounds like a vowel, while the second and third **u**'s sound like **yu**.

Following are rare cases. In the first words, **i** makes a **y** sound. In the last words, **o** includes a **w** sound.

onion / union / once / one

On pages 39 and 26, we saw how **u** can make a **w** sound.

1. Circle the words that include a **k** sound.

took / king / knot / block / blink

2. Circle the words that include a **z** sound.

zone / pizza / amazing / anxious / xerox

3. Circle the words that include a **zh** sound.

zoo / maze / azure / pretzel / seizure

4. Circle the words that include an **s** sound.

amaze / exam / pizza / pretzel / anxiety

5. Circle the words that include a **ks** sound.

fox / taxes / example / expect / anxiety

6. Circle the words that include a **gz** sound.

tax / exact / examine / exceed / anxious

7. Circle the words that include a consonant **y** sound.

until / your / young / usually / beyond

8. Circle the words that include a consonant **w** sound.

one / own / once / onion / union

SILENT CONSONANTS

Silent b: comb / thumb / subtle / limb / debt

Silent c: scent / acquire / muscle / yacht / indict

Silent d: adjective / handsome / Wednesday

Silent g: sign / design / assign / foreign / gnaw

Silent gh: light / eight / bright / thought

Silent h: ghost / echo / chaos / school / honor

Silent k: knee / know / knit / knock / knight

Silent l: talk / walk / calf / could / should

Silent n: autumn / column / hymn / solemn

Silent p: receipt / raspberry / psychology

Silent r: February

Silent s: island / aisle / debris

Silent t: castle / listen / fasten / whistle

Silent w: two / who / wrist / wrong / sword

Each word below is missing a silent consonant. Circle the answer that correctly fills in the blank.

1. _rote

g / h / k / r / w

2. cha_k

c / k / l / n / w

3. k_ob

c / h / k / l / n

4. strai__t

g / h / gh / gn / hg

5. sc_olar

c / h / k / r / w

6. wres_le

d / l / r / s / t

7. lam_

b / d / h / m / n

CONSONANT LIST

Let's quickly review the main consonant sounds.

Practice pronouncing each word a few times.

bee	pet
cat / ice	queen
dog	red
fish	see / rose
go / age	to
hat	very
jet	win
kid	fix
let	yes
me	zero
no	

The **c**, **g**, and **s** have two examples because these individual letters often make multiple sounds.

SPECIAL SOUNDS

Review the following list of special sounds. Practice pronouncing each word a few times.

s like z: rose

sh: share

si like sh: mission

su like sh: sugar

si like zh: vision

su like zh: treasure

c like s: race

ch: chair

ch like sh: chef

ch like k: school

tch: watch

ce like sh: ocean

ci like sh: special

g like j: giant

g like zh: beige

gh like f: laugh

gh like g: ghost

ph like f: phone

qu like kw: quick

th like thing: think

th like that: the

ti like sh: nation

tu like ch: actual

dr: dream

tr: try

dg like j: edge

ng: sing

wr like r: write

wh like w: what

wh like h: who

f like v: of

u like w: language

u like y: unique

i like y: onion

o like w: one

DOUBLE CONSONANTS

bubble

soccer / success

puddle

office

bigger

knickknack

ball

summer

dinner

zipper

hurry

class

little

puzzle

MULTIPLE CONSONANTS

The following words have two different consonants next to one another. Practice pronouncing these words.

blue / bread / grabs

chair / back / clean / acquire / cry / act

edge / adjust / noodle / admit / dream / woods

flat / from / soft

ghost / glad / signature / green / logs

know / cooks

elbow / old / wolf / milk / almost

help / wheels / belt / wolves

amber / autumn / camp / drums

chance / under / danger / inhale / injure / pink

inquire / pens / tent / envy / lynx / bronze

phone / play / prize / keeps / kept

orbit / arc / card / large / rhinoceros / work

girl / worm / learn / harp / cars / art / carve

scoop / shape / sky / sleep / smart

snake / sport / squirt / stop / sweet

thing / title / true / cats / between

rowdy / why / owl / town / wrap / bows

except / exhale / axle / expert / exquisite / extent

The following words have three consonants in a row.

school / scream / shrink / sphere / splash

spring / strong / asks / unsweetened / wishful

thrust / earth / ninth / catch / entry / first

instant / rhythm / night / hundredth / fifth

porch / pinch / world / chrome / brings

jungle / turtle / kindly / gentle

phrase / improve / compromise / conclude

engrave / extra / exclude / explain / sixth

eighth / twelfth / inchworm

1. Circle the words that make an **s** sound.

> pencil / pens / rose / nice / music

2. Circle the words that make a **z** sound.

> prize / desert / picnics / fries / xylophone

3. Circle the words that make a **k** sound.

> can / make / knot / race / unique

4. Circle the words that make a **sh** sound.

> super / station / mission / sure / vision

5. Circle the words that make a **ch** sound.

> chef / actual / action / fortunate / school

6. Circle the words that make a **j** sound.

> jar / angel / fudge / forgive / apologize

7. Circle the words that make a **g** sound.

> gear / gentle / girl / guess / cough

8. Circle the words that make an **f** sound.

> of / off / cough / though / graph

1. Circle the words that make a **w** sound.

   what / whom / write / rewind / sandwich

2. Circle the words that make an **h** sound.

   hour / how / who / why / whole

3. Circle the words that make a **zh** sound.

   age / beige / danger / vision / treasure

4. Circle the words that make a **kw** sound.

   quick / quiet / request / unique / mosquito

5. Circle the words that make a **th** sound like **thing**.

   this / that / breath / breathe / without

6. Circle the words that make a **th** sound like **that**.

   thin / these / bath / bathe / within

7. Circle the words that make a consonant **y** sound.

   under / unit / yes / eye / today

8. In each word, circle the consonants that are silent.

knight / thumbs / through / honorary / eighty-two

PART 2

PRONOUNCING

VOWELS

LONG VOWEL SOUNDS

Each vowel can make a long vowel sound or a short vowel sound. The long vowel sound is the same as the name of the letter:

- Hear the long **a** sound in the following words:

    rain / play / they / make / eight

- Hear the long **e** sound in the following words:

    me / see / team / key / needy

- Hear the long i sound in the following words:

    I / try / time / night / pie

- Hear the long **o** sound in the following words:

    no / boat / phone / grow / toe

- Hear the long **u** sound in the following words:

    new / tune / moon / true / through / lose

SHORT VOWEL SOUNDS

The short vowel sounds don't sound the same as the name of the letter:

- Hear the short **a** sound in the following words:

    cat / had / nap / fan / and

- Hear the short **e** sound in the following words:

    bed / egg / wet / nest / ready

- Hear the short i sound in the following words:

    is / gym / built / women / business

- Hear the short **o** sound in the following words:

    hot / fox / bother / calm / car / heart

- Hear the **aw** sound in the following words:

    saw / taught / long / ball / talk

- Hear the short **u** sound in the following words:

    cup / bus / ton / blood / trouble

- Hear the (short) **oo** sound in the following words:

book / foot / bush / could / wolf

- Hear the soft **uh** sound in the following words:

ago (a) / item (e) / cousin (i)

carrot (o) / circus (u) / vinyl (y)

Some of these short vowel sounds are very similar, yet they are a little different. For example, listen for the differences in the following words:

cup (short u) / circus (soft uh) / bury (short e)

busy (short i) / bush (short oo)

The short **o** sound and the **aw** sound are very similar:

stop (short o) / song (aw sound)

hot (short o) / hall (aw sound)

The soft **uh** sound is similar to the short **u** sound, but the soft **uh** is a weak unstressed syllable in words with multiple syllables. Compare **cup** to **circus.**

VOWEL PATTERNS

The way to pronounce vowels depends in part on the type of pattern that the vowel appears in.

- Some vowel teams make special sounds. For example, the vowel team **ai** makes a long **a** sound (like **rain**) and the vowel team **oi** makes a special sound (like **oil**).

- The silent **e** pattern has a single vowel followed by a consonant followed by an **e**, like the examples below. The **e** at the end is silent. The purpose of the silent **e** is to make the previous vowel sound long.

  mak|e| / thes|e| / tim|e| / phon|e| / tun|e|

- A single vowel by itself (without a silent **e** coming later) is usually short (like **cat** and **fun**). However, a single vowel can sometimes make multiple sounds. For example, compare **cat**, **ball**, and **ago**.

AI AND AY

The vowel teams **ai** and **ay** almost always make the long **a** sound.

say / days / stayed / playing / today

aim / brain / paid / trail / maintain

There are a few rare cases where **ai** or **ay** make a short vowel sound:

said (short e, like red)

says (short e, like red)

plaid (short a, like glad)

again (short e, like ten)

1. Circle the words that make the long **a** sound.

pays / says / stays / played / saying

2. Circle the words that make the long **a** sound.

said / paid / plaid / drain / against

EE AND EA

The vowel team **ee** almost always makes the long **e** sound.

bee / peek / seed / wheel / teeth

Following is a rare case where **ee** makes a different vowel sound:

been (short i, like win)

The vowel team **ea** often makes the long **e** sound.

each / seat / teach / beat / dream

However, sometimes **ea** makes the short **e** sound:

bread / heavy / feather / health / pleasant

Rarely, **ea** makes the long **a** sound:

break (long a, like bake)

great (long a, like gate)

How do you know whether **ea** will make the long **e** sound or short **e** sound (or even a long **a** sound)? Unfortunately, there isn't a reliable rule to help pronounce **ea** correctly. You just need to be familiar with **ea** words and remember them. Following are more examples where **ea** makes the long **e** sound.

tea / meal / bead / scream / breathe

Following are more examples where **ea** makes the short **e** sound.

head / meant / wealth / spread / breath

1. Circle the words that make the long **e** sound.

    feel / been / seen / needle / cheetah

2. Circle the words that make the long **e** sound.

    eat / steam / steak / streak / thread

EI, IE, AND EY

The vowel team **ey** usually makes the long **e** sound.

key / valley / money / monkey / journey

Occasionally, **ey** makes the long **a** sound:

they / grey / obey / survey / convey

Following is a rare case where **ey** makes the long **i** sound:

eye (long i, like try)

When the vowel team **ei** follows the letter **c**, it usually makes a long **e** sound.

ceiling / receipt / deceit / deceive / perceive

When **ei** doesn't follow a **c**, it often makes the long **a** sound.

beige / vein / eight / reins / neighbor

However, occasionally **ei** makes the long **e** sound even when it doesn't follow a **c**.

weird / seize / either / neither / leisure

Rarely, when **ei** comes at the end of a word with multiple syllables, it makes the short i sound.

forfeit / foreign / counterfeit

When a verb ends with **–eing**, the **e** and i usually make two separate vowel sounds.

being = be + ing / seeing = see + ing

Following is a rare case where **ei** makes the long i sound:

height (long i, like right)

The vowel team **ie** often makes the long **e** sound.

brief / field / niece / movie / believe

Sometimes **ie** makes the long i sound. This often happens with verbs (action words).

lie / cries / cried / tried / tries

When **ie** comes after a **c**, it almost never makes the long **e** sound. One exception is the word **species**, which does make a long **e** even though **ie** follows a **c**.

ancient (soft uh) / sufficient (soft uh)

When the **e** is part of a suffix like **–er**, **–est**, or **–ence**, the **i** and **e** often make two separate vowel sounds.

fancier = fancy + er / science = sci + ence

1. Circle the words that make the long **e** sound.

vein / weird / neither / foreign / receive

2. Circle the words that make the long **e** sound.

tie / piece / field / applies / relief

3. Circle the words that make the long **a** sound.

beige / weight / height / ceiling / neighbor

4. Circle the words that make the long **i** sound.

pier / flies / pastries / denies / believe

AU, AW, AND EW

The vowel teams **au** and **aw** almost always make the **aw** sound. Exceptions include **laugh** (short **a**), **gauge** (long **a**), and **because** (often pronounced with a short **u**).

paw / claw / lawn / straw / awkward

cause / fault / launch / vault / sauce

The vowel team **ew** almost always makes the long **u** sound. One exception is the word **sew**, which makes the long **o** sound.

new / stew / dew / shrewd / brew

Occasionally, **ew** includes a consonant **y** sound along with the long **u** sound.

few / spew / skew / nephew / curfew

---

1. Circle the words that make the **aw** sound.

law / draw / drew / faucet / laughter

io

The vowel team **io** almost always makes the soft **uh** sound. This is very common with multi-syllable words ending with **–sion** and **–tion**. We will explore the soft **uh** sound more in Chapter 3.

vision / passion / motion / action / rational

Following is a rare case where **io** makes the long **o** sound:

ratio (long o)

Occasionally, the letters **io** make two separate vowel sounds.

lion (long i + soft uh)

ionic (long i + short o)

radio (long e + long o)

---

1. Circle the words that make the soft **uh** sound.

mission / nation / studio / fictional / bionic

OA AND OE

The vowel teams **oa** and **oe** almost always make the long **o** sound.

road / coat / soap / goat / toast

toe / doe / goes / heroes / potatoes

Following is a rare case where **oa** makes the **aw** sound:

broad (aw like wrong)

Rarely, **oe** makes a different vowel sound:

shoe (long u, like suit)

does (short u, like buzz)

canoe (long u, like new)

---

1. Circle the words that make the long **o** sound.

boat / goal / foamy / abroad / approach

2. Circle the words that make the long **o** sound.

toe / echoes / doesn't / horseshoe / tomatoes

OI AND OY

The vowel teams **oi** and **oy** almost always make the **oi** sound.

boil / noise / point / coiled / joining

joy / toys / enjoy / oyster / destroying

Occasionally, the letters **oi** make two separate vowel sounds.

going (long o + short i)

Rarely, **oi** makes a different sound:

choir (long i)

tortoise (soft uh)

---

1. Circle the words that make the **oy** sound.

join / doing / porpoise / moisture / tortoise

2. Circle the words that make the **oy** sound.

boy / annoy / loyal / voyage / royalty

#

The vowel team **oo** sometimes makes the (short) **oo** sound like **book**. This often occurs before the letter **k**, occasionally before **d**, and once in a while before **t**. It rarely happens before other letters. Exceptions include **wool** and **hoof**.

look / shook / good / wood / foot

Sometimes **oo** makes the long **u** sound like **soon**. This often happens when the double **oo** doesn't come before a **k**, **d**, or **t**. Exceptions include **food**, **tooth**, and **shoot**.

noon / spoon / boot / loose / choose

Rarely, **oo** makes the short **u** sound like **cup**.

blood / flood / bloody / flooded

When it comes before the letter **r, oo** usually sounds similar to a long **o** (though for technical reasons it is classified as **aw + r),** which is the same sound as the words **more** and **store**. One exception is the word **poor,** which makes the (short) **oo** sound instead.

door / floor

1. Circle the words that make the (short) **oo** sound.

   wool / tools / sooner / wooden / bookcase

2. Circle the words that make the long **u** sound.

   food / took / nook / booth / mushroom

3. Circle the words that make the short **u** sound.

   foot / soon / bloody / loosely / flooding

4. Circle the words that make any of the following sounds: the **aw** sound, the short **o**, or the long **o**.

   tool / boots / poorly / flooring / doorknob

Note: Not every teacher or author uses the same language or notation. If you are also using another book or if you are working with a teacher, note the following:

- Some books refer to **"long oo"** and **"short oo."**

- In this book, what we call the long **u** sound is the same as what others call the long **oo** sound.

    new / tune / moon / true / through / lose

- In this book, what we call the **oo** sound is the same as what others call the short **oo** sound.

    book / bush / could / wolf / cure

OU

The letters **ou** can make eight different sounds:

- The **ow** sound like **cow**.

    out / found / our

- The long **o** sound like **no**.

    though / soul / shoulder

- The long **u** sound like **new**.

    you / group / through

- The **aw** sound like **claw**.

    cough / bought / fought

- The short **u** sound like **cup**.

    rough / cousin / young

- The soft **uh** sound like the **u** in **circus**.

    famous / nervous / serious

- The (short) **oo** sound like **good**.

    could / would / should

- Part of the **ir** sound like **turn**.

    courage / journey / journal

The following words have similar spelling, yet make several different vowel sounds.

tough (short u like cup)

though (long o like no)

through (long u like new)

thought (aw like claw)

thorough (ir like turn then long o like no)

throughout (long u like new then ow like cow)

Many **ou** words have inconsistent pronunciation:

should (oo like good) / shoulder (long o like no)

cough (aw like claw) / rough (short u like cup)

dough (long o like no) / through (long u like new)

soul (long o like no) / foul (ow like cow)

soup (long u like new) / sour (ow like cow)

The best way to remember how to pronounce **ou** words is through memory and practice.

1. Circle the words that make the long **o** sound.

   out / soul / dough / amount / southern

2. Circle the words that make the long **u** sound.

   hour / soup / count / through / journey

3. Circle the words that make the short **u** sound.

   could / young / youth / touch / cousin

4. Circle the words that make the (short) **oo** sound.

   our / house / youth / would've / shouldn't

5. Circle the words that make the soft **uh** sound.

   pout / sound / jealous / discount / precious

6. Circle the words that make the **ow** sound.

   about / shout / mouth / enough / bought

7. Circle the words that make the **aw** sound.

   cloud / mouse / tough / fought / coughing

8. Circle the words that make the **ir** sound.

   pour / sour / flour / tournament / courageous

OW

The vowel team **ow** sometimes makes the **ow** sound.

how / now / allow / vowel / anyhow

Sometimes **ow** makes the long **o** sound.

own / show / elbow / window / tomorrow

The long **o** sound is common at the end of a syllable. For example, compare **grow** (long **o**) to **growl** (ow). However, there are many exceptions. Following are examples with the **ow** sound at the end of a word.

vow / allow / eyebrow / plow / wow

Following are examples where **ow** makes the long **o** sound in the middle (or beginning) of a word.

own / bowl / known / shown / bowtie

1. Circle the words that make the long **o** sound.

power / growth / showed / shower / brownies

UE

The vowel team **ue** usually makes the long **u** sound.

blue / clue / due / true / issue

Rarely, **ue** includes a consonant **y** sound along with the long **u** sound.

value

There are a few cases where **ue** doesn't make a long **u** sound:

guest (short e)

league (silent ue)

If **ue** follows the letter **q** (like **queen**, **quest**, and **unique**), see page 39.

---

1. Circle the words that make the long **u** sound.

glued / guest / rescue / avenue / league

UI

The vowel team **ui** usually makes the long **u** sound.

fruit / juice / suit / cruise / recruit

Occasionally, **ui** makes the short i sound.

build / guilt / builder / guilty / building

Rarely, **ui** makes a different sound:

guide (long i)

suite (long e)

If **ui** follows the letter **q** (like **quick, quite,** and **liquid**), see page 39.

---

1. Circle the words that make the long **u** sound.

suite / juicy / bruise / disguise / pursuit

2. Circle the words that make the short i sound.

built / fruity / circuit / lawsuit / biscuit

VOWEL TEAMS WITH GH

A variety of vowel teams include a silent **gh.**

The vowel team **igh** almost always makes the long **i** sound (with **gh** silent).

high / fight / bright / sight / delight

The vowel team **eigh** almost always makes the long **a** sound (with **gh** silent). Exceptions include **height** and **sleight,** which make the long **i** sound instead.

eight / neighbor / weigh / freight / weight

The vowel team **aigh** makes the long **a** sound (with **gh** silent). This vowel team is rare.

straight

The vowel team **augh** almost always makes the **aw** sound (with **gh** silent).

caught / taught / naughty / daughter

An unusual case is the word **laugh,** where **au** makes the short **a** sound and **gh** makes the **f** sound.

The vowel team **ough** can make a variety of sounds:

- the **aw** sound (with **gh** silent) like **saw.** However, in the word **cough,** the **gh** makes the **f** sound.

bought / brought / fought

- the **ow** sound (with **gh** silent) like **cow.** This is rare.

drought

- the long **o** sound (with **gh** silent) like **go.**

dough / though

- the long **u** sound (with **gh** silent) like **new.**

through

- the short **u** sound (with **gh** making the **f** sound) like **stuff.** Note that **gh** isn't silent in these words.

rough / tough / enough

1. Circle the words that make the long **a** sound.

   eighty / sleigh / caught / heighten / straighten

2. Circle the words that make the long i sound.

   light / weight / straight / tonight / neighborhood

3. Circle the words that make the long **o** sound.

   dough / fought / though / through / roughly

4. Circle the words that make the long **u** sound.

   ought / cough / bought / though / through

5. Circle the words that make the short **u** sound.

   tough / caught / enough / brought / thought

6. Circle the words that make the **aw** sound.

   rough / though / naughty / thought / daughter

7. Circle the words that make the **ow** sound.

   cough / dough / through / brought / drought

8. Circle the words that make the **f** sound.

   night / tough / though / enough / highlight

UNUSUAL PAIRINGS

Some vowel pairings are rare:

aardvark (aa sounds like the ea in heart)

aerobic (ae sounds like the e in merry)

pharaoh (ao sounds like the o in go)

people (eo sounds like the e in we)

leopard (eo sounds like the e in step)

leotard (eo sounds like long e + soft uh)

neutral (eu sounds like the ew in new)

vacuum (uu sounds like the u in unit)

buy (uy sounds like the y in by)

beautiful (eau sounds like the u in unit)

buoyant (uoy sounds like the oy in boy)

view (iew sounds like the ew in few)

THE SILENT E RULE

mak**e** / thes**e** / tim**e** / phon**e** / tun**e**

When the letter **e** appears at the end of a word, it is usually silent. The pattern vowel **+** consonant **+** silent **e** helps to make a long vowel sound. For example, compare the pairs of words below.

at (short a) / **ate** (long a, silent e)

rid (short i) / **ride** (long i, silent e)

not (short o) / n**ote** (long o, silent e)

us (short u) / **use** (long u, silent e)

The patterns vowel **+** consonant **+ ing** and vowel **+** consonant **+ y** similarly help to make a long vowel sound. See the examples below.

rat (short a) / r**ati**ng (long a)

tin (short i) / t**iny** (long i)

Rarely, a silent **e** helps to make a long vowel sound before a pair of consonants:

past (short a) / paste (long a)

breath (short e) / breathe (long e)

cloth (short o) / clothe (long o)

---

1. Circle the words that make the long **a** sound.

mad / made / tale / tall / crazy

2. Circle the words that make the long **e** sound.

eve / ever / serve / extreme / evening

3. Circle the words that make the long **i** sound.

ice / hint / shiny / dining / spinning

4. Circle the words that make the long **o** sound.

joke / pony / bossy / clothing / washcloth

5. Circle the words that make the long **u** sound.

duty / dusty / funny / summer / assume

SINGLE A

A single letter **a** can make a variety of sounds:

- a single **a** often makes the short **a** sound.

    dad / ran / hat / pal / act

    ladder / rabbit / backpack

- when it comes before the letters **ll**, **lk**, or **lt** a single **a**

    often makes the **aw** sound like **saw**.

    call / halt / talk / wall / walk

- rarely, a single **a** makes the short **o** sound like **hot**.

    father / want / swap / calm

- the **a_e**, **a_i**, and **a_y** rules usually make the long **a**.

    ate / cake / maze / making / baby

- an unstressed syllable (in a multi-syllable word)

    often makes the soft **uh** sound like the **u** in **circus**.

    about / again / comma / machine cereal

- rarely, a single **a** makes the long **a** sound before two consonants. This happens more with certain letter patterns, such as **ange**, **aste**, and **able**. However, not all words with these patterns make the long **a**. Exceptions include **anger** (short **a**), **faster** (short **a**), and **suitable** (soft **uh**).

bass (music) / taste / cable / change / staple

- rarely, a single **a** makes the short **e** sound like **bed**.

any / many

- rarely, a single **a** makes the short **u** sound like **cup**.

was

- the **–al** ending after a **d** or **t** usually has a much reduced vowel sound (like an abbreviated **uh**).

tidal / vital

- when the letter **a** comes before the letter **r** (forming **ar**), it often sounds different. See page 106.

- for common prefixes and suffixes involving a single **a**, see Part 3.

---

1. Circle the words that make the long **a** sound.

   can / cane / anger / danger / making

2. Circle the words that make the short **a** sound.

   and / man / woman / table / space

3. Circle the words that make the **aw** sound.

   all / was / ball / chalk / vocal

4. Circle the words that make the short **o** sound.

   any / calm / call / swap / father

5. Circle the words that make the short **u** sound.

   has / can't / hasn't / wasn't / haven't

6. Circle the words that make the soft **uh** sound.

   alone / final / lovable / scary / summary

7. Circle the words that make the short **e** sound.

   many / zany / nanny / anybody / fantastic

SINGLE E

A single letter **e** can make a variety of sounds:

- a single **e** often makes the short **e** sound.

  ten / bell / pet / desk / next

- the **e_e**, **e_i**, and **e_y** rules usually make the long **e**.

  these / eve / scenic / defy / extreme

- a single **e** sometimes makes the long **e** sound at the

  end of a short word or prefix (like **be–** or **pre–**).

  me / she / become / between / preschool

- a single **e** can make the short **i** sound like **in**. This

  often happens with prefix **re–**, but is otherwise rare.

  pretty / women / relax / return / review

- an unstressed syllable (in a multi-syllable word)

  often makes the soft **uh** sound like the **u** in **circus**.

  item / select / happen / couple / statement

- multi-syllable words ending with **–et** usually make the long **a**. However, a few words like **wallet** make the soft **uh** sound.

   ballet / valet / filet / gourmet / ricochet

- the **–le** and **–en** endings after a **d** or **t** usually have a much reduced vowel sound (an abbreviated **uh**).

   little / middle / kitten / sudden / sweeten

- when **–ed** is added to a verb that normally ends with a **d** or **t**, it adds an extra syllable to the verb, which is pronounced **id**. (Note how the words below sound like **hid**, and don't sound like **red**.)

   folded / voted / tasted / graded / knotted

- when the letter **e** comes before the letter **r** (forming **er**), it often sounds different. See pages 104 and 107.

- for common prefixes and suffixes involving a single **e**, see Part 3.

1. Circle the words that make the long **e** sound.

he / them / tennis / delete / beware

2. Circle the words that make the long **e** sound.

we / wet / we've / preview / concrete

3. Circle the words that make the short **e** sound.

them / theme / spent / pretty / prefix

4. Circle the words that make the short **e** sound.

sled / acted / kicked / dressed / folded

5. Circle the words that make the long **a** sound.

let / valet / mallet / wallet / gourmet

6. Circle the words that make the soft **uh** sound.

panel / ballet / staple / absent / celebrate

7. Circle the words that make the short i sound.

men / women / messy / prettiest / gentlemen

8. Circle the words that make the short i sound.

handed / hiked / seated / shopped / greeted

SINGLE I

A single letter i can make a variety of sounds:

- a single i often makes the short i sound.

  big / hit / this / stick / visit

- the **i_e, i_i,** and **i_y** rules usually make the long i.

  ice / time / writing / shiny / bicycle

- occasionally, a single i makes the long i sound before two consonants or at the end of a syllable in a multi-syllable word. This happens in some words ending with **–ind** or **–ild,** for example.

  I / mind / kind / child / wild / climb

  final / pilot / rival / pirate / virus

- an unstressed syllable (in a multi-syllable word) often makes the soft **uh** sound like the **u** in **circus.**

  pencil / verify / identify / curiosity / heritage

- rarely, a single i makes the long **e** sound like **be**. This usually happens at the end of a word.

ski / taxi / chili / Jacuzzi / zucchini (both i's)

- when the letter i comes before the letter r (forming ir), it may sound different. See pages 104 and 108.

- for common prefixes and suffixes involving a single i, see Part 3.

---

1. Circle the words that make the long i sound.

wild / will / tiger / dining / winning

2. Circle the words that make the short i sound.

tin / tiny / mild / children / spaghetti

3. Circle the words that make the long e sound.

hi / him / taxicab / invisible / pepperoni

4. Circle the words that make the soft **uh** sound.

excite / notify / holiday / politics / terrible

SINGLE O

A single letter **o** can make a variety of sounds:

- a single **o** sometimes makes the short **o** sound.

  hop / rock / bottle / honest / constant

- a single **o** sometimes makes the **aw** sound like **saw**.

  This often happens before the letters **ng**.

  song / wrong / along

- a single **o** sometimes makes the short **u** sound.

  won / son / done / come / above

- a single **o** sometimes makes the long **u** sound. This often occurs before **m**, **v**, **s**, or at the end of a word (but exceptions include **go, come,** and **above**).

  do / who / whom / move / lose

- the **o_e**, **o_i**, and **o_y** rules usually make the long **o**.

  rose / note / zone / pony / hoping

- a single **o** sometimes makes the long **o** sound at the end of a syllable or short word (but not **do** or **who**).

  go / total / ago / oval / program

- when it comes before the letter **l**, a single **o** often makes the long **o** sound.

  gold / cold / fold / bolt / revolt

- occasionally, a single **o** makes the long **o** sound before two consonants or at the end of a syllable in a multi-syllable word. This happens in some words ending with **–ost**, for example.

  both / most / post / gross / almost

  over / donut / noble / protest

- an unstressed syllable (in a multi-syllable word) often makes the soft **uh** sound like the **u** in **circus**.

  c⃞o⃞rrect / li⃞o⃞n / idi⃞o⃞t / ⃞o⃞ccasion / doct⃞o⃞r

- rarely, a single **o** makes the short **i** sound like **in**.

women

- rarely, a single **o** makes the (short) **oo** sound like

book.

wolf

- the **–on** ending after a **d** or **t** usually has a much

reduced vowel sound (like an abbreviated **uh**).

button / carton / pardon

- when the letter **o** comes before the letter r (forming

or), it often sounds different. See pages 104 and 107.

- for common prefixes and suffixes involving a single

o, see Part 3.

Note: Although most words have a single correct

pronunciation, some words can be pronounced either

with the **aw** sound or the short **o** sound.

cloth (aw or short o) / hot (short o) / long (aw)

1. Circle the words that make the long **o** sound.

   not / told / cozy / prove / hoping

2. Circle the words that make the short **o** sound.

   hot / host / hotel / today / shock

3. Circle the words that make the **aw** sound.

   son / gone / nosy / strong / belong

4. Circle the words that make the long **u** sound.

   no / undo / glove / proven / hairdo

5. Circle the words that make the short **u** sound.

   done / don't / shovel / remove / sponge

6. Circle the words that make the soft **uh** sound.

   police / reason / rotate / decorate / originate

7. Circle the words that make the short **i** sound.

   body / wrote / woman / women / moment

8. Circle the words that make the (short) **oo** sound.

   golf / wolf / sold / ghost / wolves

SINGLE U

A single letter **u** can make a variety of sounds:

- a single **u** sometimes makes the short **u** sound.

  sun / duck / nut / shrug / bucket

- a single **u** occasionally makes the (short) **oo** sound.

  put / full / push / pull / sugar

- the **u_e**, **u_i**, and **u_y** rules usually make the long **u**.

  tube / super / ruby / assuming / dutiful

- sometimes, the **u_e**, **u_i**, and **u_y** rules include a

  consonant **y** + long **u**.

  cube / huge / mute / costume / confused

  puny / music / cupid / amusing / mutiny

- some words that begin with **u** also include a

  consonant **y** + long **u**.

  used / unique / usual / unit / union

- the prefix **un** almost always makes the short **u.**

undo / under / untie / uncle / unbelievable

- at the end of a syllable, a single **u** often makes the long **u** sound (the second row below includes a **y**).

flu / tuna / lunar / tuba / brutal

future / human / fuel / humor / accumulate

- an unstressed syllable (in a multi-syllable word) often makes the soft **uh** sound like the **a** in **ago.**

u̲pon / su̲ppose / bu̲rrito / cactu̲s / measu̲re

- rarely, a single **u** makes the short **e** sound like **bed.**

bury

- rarely, a single **u** makes the short **i** sound like **in.**

busy

- if the letter **u** comes after the letter **q** (forming **qu**), see page 39.

- if the letter **u** comes after the letter **g** (forming **gu**), see page 26.

- if the letter **u** comes after the letter **s** (forming **su**), see page 20.

- if the letter **u** comes after the letter **t** (forming **tu**), see page 34.

- when the letter **u** comes before the letter **r** (forming **ur**), it often sounds different. See pages 104 and 108.

- for common prefixes and suffixes involving a single **u**, see Part 3.

1. Circle the words that make the long **u** sound.

   duty / dusty / lucky / lunatic / parachute

2. Circle the words that make the long **u** sound.

   tutor / junior / jungle / ruling / pulling

3. Circle the words that make the short **u** sound.

   bus / busy / truth / unite / unlike

4. Circle the words that make the consonant **y** sound.

   mule / united / excuse / produce / humorous

5. Circle the words that make the soft **uh** sound.

   bonus / circus / dispute / spatula / century

6. Circle the words that make the short **e** sound.

   but / put / sugar / burial / buried

7. Circle the words that make the short i sound.

   full / busily / buzzer / business / beautiful

8. Circle the words that make the (short) **oo** sound.

   bush / rude / album / study / pudding

SINGLE Y

A single letter **y** can make a variety of sounds:

- a single **y** usually makes a long **i** at the end of a word with one syllable. If a vowel comes before the **y** (like **day** or **key**), see page 60, 63, or 69.

by / cry / why / try / sly

- a single **y** usually makes a long **e** at the end of a word with two or more syllables. Exceptions include **deny** and **retry**, which make the long **i**. If a vowel comes before the **y** (like **today** or **monkey**), see page 60, 63, or 69.

baby / happy / funny / mommy / daddy

- a single **y** in the middle of a word often makes the short **i** sound.

myth / symbol / rhythm / typical / bicycle

- a single **y** in the middle of a word occasionally makes the long **i** sound. This often happens with the **y_e** pattern (similar to how b**ike** makes the long **i**).

t**yp**e / st**yl**e / motorcycle

- a single **y** usually sounds like a consonant when it begins a syllable (see page 43).

- an unstressed syllable (in a multi-syllable word) can make the soft **uh** sound like the **u** in **circus**.

vin**y**l / s**y**ringe

1. Circle the words that make the long **e** sound.

dry / copy / apply / cryptic / country

2. Circle the words that make the long **i** sound.

gym / defy / messy / hyper / apology

3. Circle the words that make the soft **uh** sound.

reply / trophy / syntax / physics / analysis

THE IR SOUND

her / sir / word / turn / pearl

The **ir** sound includes a special vowel sound that is only heard before the **r** sound. Some dictionaries represent this sound with the symbol **ʉ** (which looks like a **u** with a bar through it) in their pronunciation keys.

Beware that many vowel **+ r** sounds are different from the **ir** sound:

were (ir sound) / where (short e + r)

stir (ir sound) / star (short o sound + r)

her (ir sound) / mother (soft uh + r)

word (ir sound) / more (o + r)

pearl (ir sound) / pear (short e + r)

The word **burner** makes both the **ir** sound and the soft **uh** + r sound: **burner = b + ir + n + soft uh + r.**

The letters **er, ir, or,** and **ur** can each make the **ir** sound.

However, these letters don't always make the **ir** sound. It's easiest to pronounce these words when you recognize them from memory. Following are examples where **er, ir, or,** and **ur** make the **ir** sound.

per / term / verge / were / jerk

girl / dirt / first / third / birth

word / work / worm / worst / worth

fur / turn / hurt / burst / purse

Following are two-syllable examples of **er, ir, or,** and **ur.**

person / certain / observe / submerge / iceberg

dirty / thirsty / confirm / thirteen / squirrel

worry / worker / worldly / worthwhile

occur / purple / turtle / burglar / surgeon

There are a few rare cases, where other letters make the ir sound:

- yr like **syrup**

- **ear** like **pearl**

- **ou** like **nourish**

Remember that **ir** is just one of many vowel **+ r** sounds:

- The most common vowel **+ r** ending sounds like a soft **uh + r**. It is most commonly spelled **–er**, like **father**, which sounds different from **her** (the **ir** sound). For more about the soft **uh + r** sound, see Part 3.

- When **or** doesn't follow a **w**, it usually sounds different from the **ir** sound in **work**. For example, **or** sounds similar to the long **o + r** in **more**.

- The letters **ur** make the **y + oo + r** sound in **pure**. Note the big difference between **pure** and **purse** (which makes the **ir** sound).

VOWEL + R SOUNDS

You may notice that vowels tend to sound different when they are followed by the letter **r**. For example, compare **cute** with **cure** or **shape** with **share**.

- When what would normally be a long **a** combines with an **r**, the vowel sounds more like a short **e**.

  care / chair / their / there / bear / prayer

- When what would normally be a short **a** combines with an **r**, the vowel often sounds more like a short **o** (like the **a** in **father, want,** or **swap**). However, it can also sound more like a long **o**. For example, compare **car** (short **o**) with **war** (sounds more like a long **o**, rhymes with **more**).

  short o + r: car / farm / heart / sergeant

  more like long o + r: war / warm / swarm / warrant

106

- Whether a long **o**, short **o**, or **aw** sound combines with an **r**, the result is nearly identical. Each word below sounds like a long **o** (for technical reasons, it is considered **aw**, but if you try to make the **aw** sound when you say it, it will come out wrong: try to say long **o + r** when you pronounce these words).

  more / for / four / war / door / roar

- The **ir** sound is a distinctly different vowel **+ r** sound. This common vowel **+ r** sound can be spelled many different ways, yet the sound is the same.

  her / sir / word / turn / pearl

- The soft **uh + r** sound is very common with words that have multiple syllables. The most common ending is **–er**, but it is sometimes **–ar** or **–or**. We will explore this sound further in Part 3.

  over / dancer / singer / doctor / collar

- When what would normally be a long **e** combines with an **r,** the vowel sounds more like a short **i.** However, note that the word **here** is often pronounced with a long **e** sound.

  ear / near / here / cheer / pier

- When what would normally be a **y + long u** sound combines with an **r,** the result is more like the **y + oo** sound. Compare **cute (y + long u)** with **cure (yoo).**

  cure / pure / sure / furious / purity

- The long **i** retains the same vowel sound even when it is followed by an **r.** The long **i + r** sound is almost always spelled **ire** (one exception is **higher).**

  fire / hire / wire / admire / require

- The letters **our** can make multiple sounds.

  tour (oo) / sour (ow) / pour (o) / journal (ir)

1. Circle the words that make the **ir** sound like **sir.**

her / cure / worse / nurse / mother

2. Circle the words that make the soft **uh** sound.

actor / party / dollar / father / reverse

3. Circle the words that make a vowel sound like **care.**

hair / harm / pear / start / share

4. Circle the words that make a vowel sound like **car.**

war / hard / heart / beard / stair

5. Circle the words that make a vowel sound like **more.**

born / card / warm / sword / fourth

6. Circle the words that make a vowel sound like **here.**

near / wear / were / pier / cheer

7. Circle the words that make a vowel sound like **cure.**

burn / pure / sure / curse / purse

8. Circle the words that make a vowel sound like **fire.**

tire / choir / stair / admire / acquire

VOWELS THAT OCCASIONALLY MAKE A CONSONANT W SOUND

one / once / choir

Rarely, the letter **o** makes a sound that begins with a consonant **w** even when there isn't a **w** in the word. Compare the words in the example below.

on (short o + n) / one (w + short u + n)

Note that the word **choir** is pronounced like:

choir = kw + long i + r

SILENT VOWELS

- Silent **a**

  pleasant / aisle / musically

- Silent **e**

  have / breathe / imagine

- Silent **i**

  cruise / business

- Silent **o**

  people / rough / colonel

- Silent **u**

  guess / guitar / laugh / tongue

Each word below is missing a silent vowel. Circle the answer that correctly fills in the blank.

1. forgiv_

   a / e / i / o / u

2. bru_se

   a / e / i / o / u

3. t_ugh

   a / e / i / o / u

4. ste_lthy

   a / e / i / o / u

5. le_pard

   a / e / i / o / u

6. ju_cy

   a / e / i / o / u

7. leag_

   ea / ee / ou / oe / ue

VOWEL LIST

Let's quickly review the main vowel sounds. Practice pronouncing each word a few times.

play	hot
see	cup
pie	saw
boat	book
new	use
cat	cure
bed	oil
is	cow

1. Circle the words that make a long **a** sound.

     meat / great / train / money / survey

2. Circle the words that make a long **a** sound.

     razor / seize / height / weight / ballet

3. Circle the words that make a short **a** sound.

     camp / many / break / plaid / waste

4. Circle the words that make a short **a** sound.

     was / want / laugh / chance / chalk

5. Circle the words that make a long **e** sound.

     been / seen / before / convey / monkey

6. Circle the words that make a long **e** sound.

     ski / penny / unify / receipt / neighbor

7. Circle the words that make a short **e** sound.

     gear / gentle / girl / guess / cough

8. Circle the words that make a short **e** sound.

     said / buried / women / people / leopard

1. Circle the words that make a long i sound.

   eye / virus / visit / price / prince

2. Circle the words that make a long i sound.

   chief / denied / supply / hungry / flight

3. Circle the words that make a short i sound.

   hint / wild / myth / style / silent

4. Circle the words that make a short i sound.

   bury / busy / built / women / mystery

5. Circle the words that make a long o sound.

   do / most / grow / growl / float

6. Circle the words that make a long o sound.

   does / rosy / cargo / group / boulder

7. Circle the words that make a short o sound.

   who / son / knot / brother / father

8. Circle the words that make a short o sound.

   got / taco / done / stone / honest

1. Circle the words that make a long **u** sound.

> go / who / sew / crew / soon

2. Circle the words that make a long **u** sound.

> book / clue / juice / south / through

3. Circle the words that make a short **u** sound.

> done / under / music / bloody / double

4. Circle the words that make an **aw** sound.

> walk / strong / caught / brought / southern

5. Circle the words that make a soft **uh** sound.

> again / coupon / double / visitor / support

6. Circle the words that make a (short) **oo** sound.

> push / look / good / tooth / should

7. Circle the words that make an **oi** sound.

> toy / enjoy / spoil / noisy / choir

8. Circle the words that make an **ow** sound.

> soup / mouth / cause / eyebrow / unknown

PART 3
PRONOUNCING
SYLLABLES

COUNTING SYLLABLES

Words are divided into syllables based on the number of distinct vowel sounds. The best way to count syllables is to pronounce the word with your voice and listen to the number of distinct vowel sounds that you hear.

rainbow = rain + bow (2 syllables)

The word **rainbow** has two syllables because it makes two distinct vowel sounds:

- **rain** makes the long **a** sound (like **play**)

- **bow** makes the long **o** sound (like **no**)

exclusive = ex + clu + sive (3 syllables)

The word **exclusive** has three syllables because it makes three distinct vowel sounds:

- **ex** makes the short **e** sound (like **bed**)

- **clu** makes the long **u** sound (like **new**)

- **sive** makes the short **i** sound (like **in**)

COUNTING VOWELS

Sometimes, two vowel sounds blend together to form a single vowel sound. For example, the **oi** in **noise** makes a single vowel sound. If you pronounce the word noise slowly, you might think that you hear two separate vowel sounds, but the **oi** sound actually counts as a single (blended) vowel sound.

noise (1 syllable, just 1 distinct vowel sound)

Other times, two vowels make two distinct vowel sounds. For example, **ea** in **create** involves the long **e** sound followed by the long **a** sound made separately. The word **create** has two syllables.

create = cre + ate (2 syllables)

In comparison, the word **breathe** has a single syllable because in this case the **ea** makes the long **e** sound only.

breathe (1 syllable, just 1 distinct vowel sound)

EXAMPLES

Practice pronouncing the following words. Count the number of distinct vowel sounds that you hear.

train (1 syllable)

mouth (1 syllable)

into = in + to (2 syllables)

playing = play + ing (2 syllables)

piece (1 syllable)

pliers = pli + ers (2 syllables)

idea = i + de + a (3 syllables)

nightmare = night + mare (2 syllables)

radio = ra + di + o (3 syllables)

because = be + cause (2 syllables)

triangle = tri + ang + le (3 syllables)

universally = u + ni + ver + sal + ly (5 syllables)

1. Count the number of syllables in each word below.

outside / graded / spoiled

brought / intersect / language

garage / spaghetti / eyesight

understanding / countertop / invisibility

2. Count the number of syllables in each word below.

reason / reuse / reaction

area / flea / heavy

being / eight / weighing

ancient / science / happiest

3. Count the number of syllables in each word below.

persuasive / violent / emotional

reopen / leopard / leotard

cooperate / initial / initiation

courageous / unusual / especially

TYPES OF SYLLABLES

There are several different types of syllables:

- Closed syllables end with a consonant. The vowel sound is usually short in a closed syllable.

  puddle / misty / begin

- Open syllables end with a vowel sound. The vowel sound is usually long in an open syllable.

  paper / open / hello

- Silent **e** syllables have a silent **e** at the end that usually helps to make a long vowel sound. A silent **e** syllable may be a word, like **time** or **hope**.

  combine / anytime / hopeful

- Consonant **+ le** syllables end with a consonant plus the letters **le**.

  able / jungle / sprinkle

- Vowel team syllables have vowels working together (sometimes with silent consonants) to create a single vowel sound. For example, vowel teams include the **ea** in **team,** the **aw** in **saw,** the **ay** in **play,** the **oy** in **boy,** and the **igh** in **night.**

laugh|ter / to|day / fa|mous|ly

- Vowel **+ r** syllables have an **r** following a vowel. The vowel usually sounds different from normal when it is followed by an **r.** For example, compare the sounds of **car** and **cat** or **first** and **fist.**

ar|my / doc|tor / re|gard|less

Each type of syllable is based on the vowel sound. Understanding how a word can be broken down into syllables can sometimes help you pronounce a word. This doesn't provide a foolproof way to pronounce words, but the clues can be helpful sometimes. Let's explore how.

For example, compare the following two-syllable words. The words on the first line begin with closed syllables with short vowel sounds, while the words on the second line begin with open syllables with long vowel sounds. Do you see a pattern?

fas|ter / pret|ty / dig|ging / lon|gest / luc|ky

sha|dy / e|ven / pi|lot / ro|ses / tu|na

- When a closed syllable doesn't come at the end of a word, there are usually at least two consonants between the vowel sounds. Note how the double **t** in **pretty** and the double **g** in **digging** help to prevent the first vowel from making a long sound.

- When an open syllable doesn't come at the end of a word, there is often just one consonant between the vowel sounds. The consonant following the open syllable isn't doubled in order to help the first vowel sound long.

You can see this difference in the following examples. The word on the left begins with a closed syllable, while the word on the right begins with an open syllable.

din|ner (short i) / di|ner (long i)

hop|ping (short o) / ho|ping (long o)

sup|per (short u) / su|per (long u)

This doesn't just happen with double consonants (like **nn** and **pp**). The following example illustrates the same idea with **ck** compared to a soft **c**.

pac|king (hard ck) / pa|cing (soft c)

For similar reasons, there is often just a single consonant before the **e** in silent **e** syllables in order to make a long vowel sound. See the consonants **t**, **s**, and **c** that come before a silent **e** in the examples below.

re|late| / sur|prise| / nice|ly

There is a similar difference between open and closed syllables when they are followed by consonant **+ le** syllables. In the examples below, the word on the left begins with a closed syllable, while the word on the right begins with an open syllable.

bab|ble (short a) / ca|ble (long a)

lit|tle (short i) / ti|tle (long i)

gob|ble (short o) / no|ble (long o)

snug|gle (short u) / bu|gle (long u)

However, there are exceptions to these rules. Following are a few examples of exceptions.

hon|est (short o, n not doubled)

tri|ple (short i, p not doubled)

strol|ler (long o, double l)

mind|ful (long i, multiple consonants)

1. Circle the closed syllables in the words below.

   mango / messy / basic / accept / tangle

2. Circle the open syllables in the words below.

   cable / fusion / polo / cargo / rising

3. Circle the closed syllables in the words below.

   bewildered / personal / triangle / diversion

4. Circle the open syllables in the words below.

   newspaper / delightful / dilated / invasion

5. Circle the silent **e** syllables in the words below.

   hopeful / lifetime / primate / televise / reuse

6. Circle the consonant **+ le** syllables in the words below.

   staple / buckle / puddle / turtle / bottleneck

7. Circle the vowel team syllables in the words below.

   enjoy / raisin / discount / laughter / shoulder

8. Circle the vowel **+ r** syllables in the words below.

   carpet / dollar / gourmet / stroller / harder

PREFIXES AND SUFFIXES

A prefix is a syllable joined to the beginning of a word, like the **be** of **beside.** A suffix is a syllable joined to the end of a word, like the **able** of **capable.** Many words with multiple syllables include one or more prefixes and suffixes, like the following examples.

re–place

- the prefix **re–** means to put back

- **place** means a specific location

- **re + place = replace,** meaning to put something back in its place

quick–ly

- **quick** means fast

- the suffix **–ly** means in the manner of

- **quick + ly = quickly,** meaning in a fast manner

pre–view

- the prefix **pre–** means before

- **view** means to see

- **pre + view = preview,** meaning to show before

un–real

- the prefix **un–** means not

- **real** means actual

- **un + real = unreal,** meaning not actual

joy–ful

- **joy** means happiness

- the suffix **–ful** means full of

- **joy + ful = joyful,** meaning full of happiness

sub–way

- the prefix **sub–** means below

- **way** means a path

- **sub + way = subway,** a path below ground

COMMON PREFIXES

Following are some examples of common prefixes:

- **re–** means again, like **refill** (to fill again)

- **pre–** means before, like **preset** (to set before)

- **un–** means not, like **unfair** (not fair)

- **dis–** means the opposite, like **disagree** (not agree)

- **in–** means not, like **invisible** (not visible)

- **ex–** means out, like **exchange** (to switch out)

- **mis–** means wrongly, like **misuse** (to use wrongly)

- **con–** means together, like **contract** (draw together)

- **anti–** means against, like **antisocial** (against society)

- **de–** means away from, like **deposit** (to put away)

- **ab–** means away, like **absent** (away)

- **inter–** means between, like **interfere** (come between)

- **intro–** means into, like **introduce** (to lead into)

- **bi–** means two, like **bicycle** (having two wheels)

- **tri–** means three, like **tripod** (having three feet)

- **semi–** means half, like **semiannual** (half yearly)

- **hemi–** means half, like **hemisphere** (half a sphere)

- **di–** means twice, like **divide** (split into two parts)

- **mono–** means single, like **monopoly** (single seller)

- **uni–** means one, like **uniform** (one form)

- **poly–** means many, like **polygon** (many sides)

- **sub–** means below, like **submarine** (under water)

- **super–** means above, like **superior** (higher up)

- **under–** means below, like **underline** (a line beneath)

- **over–** means above, like **overhead** (above the head)

- **para–** means beside, like **parallel** (side by side)

- **non–** means not, like **nonsense** (not making sense)

- **per–** means through, like **perhaps** (through chance)

COMMON SUFFIXES

Following are some examples of common suffixes:

- **–ly** means in the manner of, like **easily** (with ease)

- **–ous** means having, like **famous** (having fame)

- **–al** means relating to, like **naval** (relating to navy)

- **–ive** means characterized by, like **massive** (much mass)

- **–y** means characteristic of, like **messy** (like a mess)

- **–ful** means full of, like **beautiful** (full of beauty)

- **–less** means without, like **thoughtless** (no thought)

- **–ness** means state of, like **kindness** (a kind state)

- **–ity** means state of, like **reality** (state of being real)

- **–ic** means like, like **angelic** (like an angel)

- **–ish** means similar to, like **foolish** (like a fool)

- **–en** means to make, like **soften** (to make softer)

- **–able** means can, like **useable** (can be used)

- **–tion** means act, like **reaction** (act of reacting)

- **–ment** means act, like **agreement** (act of agreeing)

- **–dom** means state of, like **freedom** (a free state)

- **–ship** means state of, like **friendship** (a friendly state)

- **–er** means more, like **wiser** (having more wisdom)

- **–est** means most, like **wisest** (most wise)

- **–ify** means to make, like **unify** (to make into one)

- **–ize** means to make, like **realize** (to make real)

- **–ate** means to make, like **dilate** (to make wider)

- **–ed** means in the past, like **lied** (a lie already told)

- **–ing** means presently, like **running** (run now)

- **–es** means plural, like **boxes** (more than one box)

- **–or** means one who does, like **actor** (one who acts)

- **–ist** means one who does, like **artist** (who makes art)

- **–ology** means study of, like **biology** (study of life)

COMMON ROOTS

Following are some examples of common roots:

- **vis** means see, like **vision** and **televise**

- **port** means carry, like **portable** and **transport**

- **struct** means build, like **structure** and **construct**

- **gram** means written, like **grammar** and **diagram**

- **loc** means place, like **local** and **relocate**

- **vers** means turn, like **version** and **reverse**

- **sect** means cut, like **section** and **dissect**

- **form** means shape, like **formulate** and **reform**

- **lab** means work, like **labor** and **elaborate**

- **tract** means pull, like **tractor** and **distract**

- **log** means word, like **logic** and **illogical**

- **mand** means order, like **mandate** and **command**

- **voc** means voice, like **vocal** and **advocate**

WORD BUILDING

Many words with multiple syllables are built by adding prefixes or suffixes together with roots.

ex + port + ed = exported

- the prefix **ex–** means out

- the root **port** means to carry

- the suffix **–ed** means in the past

For example, **ex–**, **port**, and **–ed** combine together to make the word **exported.** If you put the separate meanings of **ex–** and **port** together, you get **export**, which means "carry out." If you add the meaning of **–ed** to **export**, you get the past tense, which is "carried out." The word **exported** actually means "sent to another country," which equates to "carried out" in the sense that goods are being carried out of the country.

Following are a few examples:

inter + sect = intersect

in + form + ed = informed

voc + al + ize = vocalize

con + tract + or = contractor

re + con + struct + ing = reconstructing

Beware that prefixes, roots, and suffixes occasionally change spelling when forming words with multiple syllables. When this happens, it usually helps the word sound or look better. Following are some examples.

- in + form + tion = inform**a**tion (gains an **a**)

- con + struct + tion = construc**t**ion (two t's merge)

- re + vers + able = revers**i**ble (an **a** changes to an i)

- in + mobile = i**m**mobile (an n changes to an **m**)

- con + vers = convers**e** (gains a silent **e**)

- ab + tract = ab**s**tract (gains an **s**)

Ordinary words can serve as roots, too:

color + ful = colorful

un + real = unreal

de + light + ed = delighted

Note that if you combine the meanings of the prefixes, suffixes, and root word together, the result may be somewhat different from the actual meaning of the word. For example, if you combine the prefix **non–** (meaning not) with the root **plus** (meaning more) to make **nonplus**, you probably wouldn't guess what the word **nonplus** actually means: "so perplexed that one is unable to speak." (However, once you know the actual definition, you may be able to see how it relates to the prefix and root. In this case, "not" + "more" means that you can't speak any more. In this example, the difficulty is that "speaking" isn't conveyed by the meaning of the prefix or the root.)

Note that prefixes and suffixes (and even roots) sometimes have multiple meanings. For example, the prefix **de–** can mean a few different things:

- In **derail**, the prefix **de–** means "away from"

- In **degrade**, the prefix **de–** means "down"

- In **defrost**, the prefix **de–** means "undo"

A prefix occasionally serves as an intensive, which means that it intensifies (adds strength to) the meaning. For example, while the prefix **dis–** means "opposite" in **dissatisfied** (which means not satisfied), the prefix instead serves as intensive in **disgruntled** (which means displeased and sulky, intensifying the negative emotion conveyed in a **grunt** rather than making it mean the opposite). As another example, the prefix **in–** means "not" in **inflexible**, but instead intensifies the meaning of "to lead" in **induce**.

1. Circle the prefixes in each of the following words.

invent / preserve / untie

recent / design / innovate

interfere / concept / exclusive

introduce / underside / improvement

2. Circle the suffixes in each of the following words.

cooler / building / apartment

thoughtful / friendly / energize

verify / capable / courageous

conditioner / sparingly / realize

3. Circle the roots in each of the following words.

defense / wildest / resist

rotate / program / measure

distraction / pretending / conversation

invisible / unworthy / excitement

unimportant / recreational / misunderstood

COMPOUND WORDS

Two ordinary words are sometimes joined together to create a compound word. For example, the words **some** and **time** combine together to make the word **sometime**. Following are examples of compound words.

rain + bow = rainbow

book + store = bookstore

every + thing = everything

Occasionally, a compound word includes a hyphen (-) or a space between the words.

ice + cream = ice-cream

up + to + date = up-to-date

merry + go + round = merry-go-round

living + room = living room

up + side + down = upside down

Break each compound word into shorter words.

1. forever

   = _____ + _____

2. downstairs

   = _____ + _____

3. bookcase

   = _____ + _____

4. upbeat

   = _____ + _____

5. yourself

   = _____ + _____

6. therefore

   = _____ + _____

7. anyone

   = _____ + _____

8. furthermore

   = _____ + _____

STRESSED SYLLABLES

When we speak, we don't pronounce every syllable of a word with the same degree of stress. (If you did, you would sound odd, like a robot.) A standard dictionary uses a stress mark (') to indicate which syllables are stressed or unstressed. For example, in the word **person** the first syllable **per** is stressed, while in the word **forget** the second syllable **get** is stressed.

per'–son (1ˢᵗ syllable is stressed)

for–get' (2ⁿᵈ syllable is stressed)

We pronounce the stressed syllable a little louder and longer than the unstressed syllable. Pronounce these words and try to hear the difference in stress.

fol'–low (1ˢᵗ syllable is stressed)

a–go' (2ⁿᵈ syllable is stressed)

for'–tune (1ˢᵗ syllable is stressed)

The word **project** can help to illustrate the difference between stressed and unstressed syllables. That's because **project** can actually be pronounced two different ways.

proj' ect (short o, 1st syllable is closed and stressed)

pro ject' (long o, 2nd syllable is closed and stressed)

As a noun, the word **project** means "something that is planned and carried out." The noun form of project is pronounced with a short **o** sound, placing stress on the first syllable. The first syllable is closed in this case.

We're working on a class proj ect together.

As a verb, the word **project** means "to cast forward." The verb form of project is pronounced with a long **o** sound, placing stress on the second syllable. The first syllable is open in this case.

Use a device to pro ject the image onto a screen.

There are a few rules to help determine which syllable is stressed in a word with two syllables:

- Two-syllable nouns usually place the stress on the first syllable. Recall that a noun is a person, place, or thing.

moth'–er / mount'–ain / shov'–el

- Two-syllable verbs often place the stress on the second syllable. Recall that a verb is typically an action word (like run, call, or wave).

ex–plore' / trans–port' / con–fuse'

- Two-syllable adjectives usually place the stress on the first syllable. Recall that an adjective typically describes a noun (like red, small, or fast).

yel'–low / ti'–ny / grate'–ful

Note that there are exceptions to these rules. For example, the word **jin'–gle** is a verb that places stress on the first syllable instead of the second.

Examine the two lists of three-syllable words below. None of these words has a long vowel sound in the middle, yet in the second row of words there is a single consonant (instead of a double consonant) before the –ing or –ed suffix.

occur'ring / begin'ning / prefer'ring / recalled'

hap'pening / but'toning / tun'neling / doc'tored

The difference has to do with stress, which is indicated by the stress marks (') in the above words.

- When the consonant is doubled before –ing or –ed, the stress falls on the second syllable. For example, the word **beginning** has a double **nn** before the –ing ending and the second syllable (**gin**) is stressed.

- When a single consonant comes before –ing or –ed, the stress falls on the first syllable. For example, the word **buttoning** has a single **n** before the –ing ending and the first syllable (**but**) is stressed.

1. Circle the stressed syllable in each word below.

father / arrange / purple

heavy / dollar / pretend

deny / quiet / planet

dentist / funny / collect

2. Circle the stressed syllable in each word below.

grumpy / explain / wallet

surround / active / person

moment / honest / prepare

carry / machine / above

3. Circle the stressed syllable in each word below.

listening / referring / mentoring

retelling / fastening / beginner

unplanned / sheltered / occurred

misspelled / fastened / happened

THE SOFT UH SOUND

<u>a</u>go (a) / it<u>e</u>m (e) / cous<u>i</u>n (i)

carr<u>o</u>t (o) / circ<u>u</u>s (u) / vin<u>y</u>l (y)

nat<u>io</u>n (io) / barg<u>ai</u>n (ai) / fam<u>ou</u>s (ou)

The soft **uh** sound is actually the most common vowel sound in the English language. It is similar to the short **u** sound, but it is softer and weaker. Many dictionaries represent the soft **uh** sound by the symbol ə, which looks like an **e** that is both upside down and backwards. For example, the pronunciation of **banana** looks like:

bə–nan'–ə

The stress mark (') indicates that the middle syllable **nan** is stressed. The unstressed syllables **bə** and **ə** each make the soft **uh** sound, whereas the stressed syllable **nan** makes the short **a** sound.

The soft **uh** sound is called the Schwa sound, and is very common in words with multiple syllables.

politics = pol'–ə–tiks'

In the example above, the thick stress mark (′) indicates the main stressed syllable, the light stress mark (') indicates a level of secondary stress, and the syllable without the stress mark is unstressed. The example below doesn't have a syllable with secondary stress: It has one syllable with main stress and two syllables that are unstressed.

syllable = sil'–ə–bəl

The soft **uh** sound is often heard in unstressed syllables. If you can identify the stressed and unstressed syllables in a word, this may help you figure out when to pronounce the soft **uh** sound. It also helps if you are familiar with common spelling patterns. We will explore a variety of soft **uh** patterns in this section.

The soft **uh** sound is sometimes spelled using a single **a**. This is common at both the beginning and the end of words, as well as some prefixes and suffixes.

a̶bout / a̶lone / a̶way / a̶head / a̶gain

tuna̶ / comma̶ / sofa̶ / drama̶ / yoga̶

ma̶chine / pa̶rade / dolla̶r / woma̶n / cerea̶l

The soft **uh** sound is sometimes spelled using a single **e**. This almost never happens with the first or last letter of a word. It is especially common with **er** and **le**.

se̶lect / happe̶n / ove̶r / couple̶ / stateme̶nt

The soft **uh** sound is sometimes spelled using a single i. This almost never happens with the first or last letter of a word. When the letter i is involved in a soft **uh** sound, it is often paired with another letter, like **capta̶in** or **moti̶on**, as we will explore later.

penci̶l / veri̶fy / identi̶fy / curiosi̶ty / heri̶tage

149

The soft **uh** sound is sometimes spelled using a single **o**.

This is common with some prefixes and suffixes, like **or**.

It occasionally also happens at the beginning of a word.

p|o|lice / c|o|rrect / li|o|n / seas|o|n / idi|o|t

|o|ffend / |o|ccasion / |o|riginate / doct|o|r

The soft **uh** sound is sometimes spelled using a single **u**.

This almost never happens with the first or last letter

of a word (but one exception is the word **upon**).

|u|pon / s|u|ppose / b|u|rrito / cact|u|s / meas|u|re

Rarely, the soft **uh** sound is spelled using a single **y**.

vin|y|l / s|y|ringe

The soft **uh** sound appears in two very common words

that have just one syllable. The word **the** is usually

pronounced with a soft **uh** sound, except when it comes

before a vowel (then it may have a long **e**, like **the end**).

|a| / th|e|

When the soft **uh** sound comes in between other syllables, it is difficult to tell which letter is used. For example, it's very common to misspell **separate** (which has an **a** between the **p** and **r**, not an **e**). It helps to memorize these words. (The hyphens are shown just to emphasize how these syllables are broken down.)

mag-a-zine / cel-e-brate / hol-i-day

dec-o-rate / spat-u-la

The soft **uh** sound is sometimes spelled as part of a vowel group. For example, the common **–tion** ending almost always makes the soft **uh** sound. Following are a variety of examples where the soft **uh** sound takes part in a vowel group.

captain / ocean / foreign / surgeon / courageous

chauffeur / special / action / precious / genius

porpoise / curious / aqueduct / requisite

The following patterns, tips, and rules sometimes help to spell the **uh** sound. When a word begins with a soft **uh** sound, it usually begins with the letter **a**. There are a few exceptions, such as **upon** and **offend**.

ago / about / alone / around / appear

When a word ends with **uh+r,** it is usually spelled **er.** Words that end with **–or** often stem from words that end with **–ct** (like **actor**), **–ate** (like **calculator**), or **–it** (like **editor**). Words that end with **–ar** often follow an **l** (like **dollar**). Comparison words (like **smaller**) end with **–er,** even if they would follow the **–or** or **–ar** pattern.

dancer / singer / camper / player / smaller

tractor / doctor / alligator / creator / visitor

dollar / collar / regular / similar / popular

Following are some exceptions to these rules.

labor / favor / color / error / sailor / altar / liar

When a word ends with **uh+r+y,** it may be spelled **ary, ery, ory,** or **ury.** If you recognize that **y** has been added to a shorter word (like **nurse + r + y = nursery** or **treasure – e + y = treasury**), this may help you figure out the spelling. For other words (like **anniversary**), it helps to memorize the spelling.

summary / anniversary

bakery / mystery / nursery / pottery / machinery

factory / memory / history / century / luxury

Words that end with **ary** often make a long **a** sound instead of a soft **uh** sound. Compare the words below.

library (long a) / summary (soft uh)

When a word ends with **uh+n,** it is often **en,** but it can be spelled **on, ain,** or **ine** (but **sh+uh+n** is often **tion**).

open / happen / listen / fallen / given

gallon / lemon / million / bargain / medicine

When a word ends with the **uh+l** sounds, it is usually spelled **le.** However, there are notable exceptions where it is instead spelled **el** or **al.** Rarely, it can even be spelled **yl** (like **vinyl**).

apple / circle / handle / puzzle / waffle

shovel / panel / local / neutral / final

When a word ends with **uh+b+uh+l,** it may be spelled **able** or **ible.** In many cases, **able** is added to a complete word. For example, compare **readable** ("read" is a word) and **terrible** ("terr" isn't a word). Sometimes a silent **e** is dropped, like notable (**note – e + able = notable**), or **y** changes to **i** (like **reliable**). However, there are exceptions, like **probable** (since **"prob"** isn't a word) and **destructible** (since "**destruct**" is a word).

suitable / transferable / lovable / adorable

horrible / audible / incredible / reversible

When a word ends with **uh+t,** it is usually spelled **ate.**

Listen carefully: Words ending with **–ite** (like **granite**), usually make a short **i** sound (like **definite**) or a long **i** sound (like **excite**) instead of a soft **uh.**

estimate / coordinate / alternate / duplicate

Actually, the previous words can be pronounced two different ways: When they are nouns, the **–ate** suffix makes a soft **uh** sound, but when they are verbs, the **–ate** suffix makes a long **a** sound (like **gate**).

Can you give me an estim⟨ate⟩? (soft uh)

Can you ⟨estimate⟩ the cost? (long a sound)

Some words with the **–ate** suffix can only be pronounced one way. For example, **certificate** is only a noun, so it ends with the soft **uh** sound, whereas **originate** is only a verb, so it ends with a long **a** sound.

When a word ends with **uh+s,** it is usually spelled **ous.**

famous / studious / gorgeous / jealous / anxious

When a syllable sounds like **sh+uh+n,** it is often **tion.**

Occasionally, it is instead spelled **sion** (like **mission).**

There are also rare exceptions like **patient.**

motion / caution / portion / correction / rational

When a word ends with **sh+uh+l,** it is usually spelled

tial after a consonant or **cial** after a vowel.

partial / essential / residential / potential

special / crucial / social / artificial / official

Following are some notable exceptions to this rule:

initial / spatial / commercial / financial

When a word ends with **uh+ns,** it may be spelled **ence** or

ance. It's difficult to tell which without memorizing it.

absence / evidence / dependence / existence

substance / appliance / allowance / significance

When a word ends with **uh+nt,** it may be spelled **ent** or **ant.** It's difficult to tell which without memorizing it. However, note that **ent/ant** words often match **ence/ance** words. For example, compare **absent** to **absence** and **significant** to **significance.**

absent / evident / dependent / existent

pleasant / instant / significant / truant

In some of the cases where the **uh** sound is involved in a group of vowels, one of the vowels actually participates in a special sound. For example, the letters **qu** make the **kw** sound, **ce** and **ci** sometimes make the **sh** sound, and **ti** sometimes makes the **sh** sound. (We discussed these and other special sounds in Part 1.) If you recognize a special consonant sound with the soft **uh** sound, this may help you spell the **uh** sound correctly. Listen for the special sounds in the following examples.

patient (ti = sh) / edition (ti = sh) / question (ti = ch)

vision (si = zh) / region (gi = j) / surgeon (ge = j)

ocean (ce = sh) / facial (ci = sh) / righteous (te = ch)

anxious (xi = sh) / acquisition (qu = kw, ti = sh)

The word **rhythm** is unusual in that it makes a soft **uh** sound where there isn't a vowel. In this example, the soft **uh** sound comes after the **th** sound and before the **m** sound. It is pronounced with two syllables.

rhythm = rith' əm

The soft uh sound can also be heard in some contractions, where an apostrophe (') indicates a missing letter. For example, **doesn't = does not.**

isn't / hasn't / doesn't / could've / should've

1. Circle the syllables that make the soft **uh** sound.

around / open / bonus

fasten / peril / nervous

agent / offense / passion

proper / parade / mention

2. Circle the syllables that make the soft **uh** sound.

animal / uniform / opposite

relative / allowance / injury

appearance / excellent / transition

holiday / history / technical

3. Circle the syllables that make the soft **uh** sound.

elevator / apology / disagreement

occasional / education / arithmetic

application / informative / biology

opportunity / harmoniously / counterproductive

1. Circle the syllables that make the soft **uh** sound.

bottom / cactus / surround

martial / avoid / comfort

listen / suggest / shuffle

collect / nature / wasn't

2. Circle the syllables that make the soft **uh** sound.

practical / visitor / century

terrible / verify / elephant

hesitant / usual / resistance

origin / avenue / production

3. Circle the syllables that make the soft **uh** sound.

analysis / intelligence / especially

certificate / originate / invisible

suspiciously / appreciate / refrigerate

astronomical / determination / miscellaneous

PART 4

SIMILAR

SOUNDS

SIMILAR CONSONANTS

It is instructive to note how very similar words can have much different pronunciation.

- Note the differences for each pair of words below.

- Practice pronouncing each word several times until you can hear the difference clearly.

- It is worth trying to memorize any words that don't come easily to you.

- Practice pronouncing any troublesome words several additional times each until you feel confident saying them.

of (v sound) / off (f sound)

lost (st sound) / lots (ts sound)

axe (ks sound) / ask (sk sound)

decks (ks sound) / desk (sk sound)

cooked (t sound) / crooked (d sound, 2 syllables)

lose (z sound) / loose (s sound)

close (z sound) the door / that was close (s sound)

music (z sound) / basic (s sound)

use (z sound) a hammer / there is no use (s sound)

puzzle (z sound) / pizza (ts sound)

missing (s sound) / mission (sh sound)

caution (sh sound) / question (ch sound)

assume (s sound) / assure (sh sound)

measure (zh sound) / sure (sh sound)

anger (g sound) / danger (j sound)

stronger (g sound) / stranger (j sound)

get (g sound) / gem (j sound)

girl (g sound) / gist (j sound)

angle (g sound) / angel (j sound)

magazine (g sound) / margarine (j sound)

whale (w sound) / whole (h sound)

tough (f sound) / though (silent gh)

thought (th like thing) / though (th like that)

thin (th like thing) / this (th like that)

breath (th like thing) / breathe (th like that)

sing (ng sound) / sign (n sound) / singe (j sound)

gone (n sound) / gong (ng sound, but no clear g)

log (clear g) / long (ng sound, but no clear g)

thin (n sound) / thing (ng sound) / think (ng + k)

cute (k sound) / cite (s sound)

chew (ch sound) / chef (sh sound)

chaps (ch sound) / chaos (k sound)

reached (ch sound) / ached (k sound)

soccer (k sound) / accept (ks sound)

nice (s sound) / ocean (sh sound)

spacing (s sound) / special (sh sound)

yes (consonant y) / eyes (vowel y)

unify (consonant y sound) / unfit (vowel u)

one (consonant w sound) / owe (vowel sound)

unique (n sound) / union (ny sound)

house (h sound) / hour (silent h)

shoulder (l sound) / should (silent l)

listed (t sound) / listen (silent t)

hand (d sound) / handsome (silent d)

swoop (sw sound) / sword (silent w)

muscular (c sound) / muscle (silent c)

costume (t sound) / fortune (ch sound)

finger (ng + clear g sound) / singer (ng, no clear g)

player (l sound, 2 syllables) / prayer (r sound, 1 syllable)

quit (kw sound) / mosquito (k sound)

baggage (g sound) / language (gw sound)

anxiety (z sound) / anxious (ksh sound)

SIMILAR VOWELS

pal (short a) / tall (aw sound)

ant (short a) / want (short u)

zany (long a) / many (short e)

has (short a) / was (short u)

past (short a) / paste (long a)

angel (long a) / angle (short a)

jagged (short a + short i) / wagged (1 syllable)

gather (short a) / father (short o)

I can estimate (long a) / it's an estimate (uh)

accept (short a) / except (short e)

desert (1st e is short) / dessert (1st e is long)

wallet (short i) / ballet (long a)

pen (short e) / pin (short i)

limb (short i) / climb (long i)

hint (short i) / pint (long i)

comb (long o) / come (short u)

bother (short o) / mother (short u)

go (long o) / do (long u)

on (short o) / ton (short u)

gone (aw sound) / done (short u)

golf (aw sound) / wolf (short oo) / gold (long o)

woman (o = short oo) / women (o = short i)

gut (short u) / put (short oo)

super (long u) / supper (short u)

brush (short u) / bush (short oo)

busy (short i like in) / bury (short e like bed)

dull (short u) / full (short oo)

tube (long u) / cube (y + long u)

unit (y + long u) / unlit (short u, no y)

entry (long e) / retry (long i)

paid (long a) / said (short e) / plaid (short a)

caught (aw sound) / laugh (short a)

cause (aw sound) / because (short u)

say (long a) / says (short e)

player (long a + uh) / prayer (short e, 1 syllable)

bead (long e) / bread (short e)

beak (long e) / break (long a)

I can read (long e) / I read it (short e)

seen (long e) / been (short i)

height (long i) / weight (long a)

new (long u) / few (y + long u)

fried (long i) / friend (short e)

pie (long i) / piece (long e)

leopard (short e) / leotard (long e + uh)

new (long u) / sew (long o)

radio (long e + long o) / ratio (long o)

road (long o) / broad (aw sound)

goes (long o) / does (short u)

boot (long u) / foot (short oo)

mood (long u) / flood (short u)

soul (long o) / soup (long u) / sour (ow sound)

you (long u) / your (short oo like poor)

youth (long u) / young (short u)

count (ow sound) / coupon (y + long u)

though (long o) / through (long u)

tough (short u + f) / thought (aw sound, silent gh)

brought (aw sound) / drought (ow sound)

soul (long o) / should (short oo like good)

county (ow sound) / country (short u)

now (ow sound) / know (long o)

glue (long u) / guest (short e)

guide (long i) / guilt (short i)

suit (long u) / suite (w + long e)

far (short o like car) / war (or like storm)

warm (or like storm) / worm (ir like sir)

staring (short e like bear) / starring (short o like car)

here (short i like pier) / there (short e like bear)

were (ir like sir) / where (short e like bear)

north (or like storm) / worth (ir like sir)

bury (short e like bear) / burn (ir like sir)

curse (ir like sir) / cure (y + short oo sound)

syrup (ir like sir) / syringe (soft uh)

chair (short e like bear) / choir (w + long i)

pear (short e like bear) / pearl (ir like girl)

hear (short i like pier) / heart (short o like car)

poor (short oo like your) / door (or like storm)

tour (oo) / sour (ow) / pour (or) / journal (ir)

flour (ow sound) / flower (ow sound + uh, 2 syllables)

PART 5
PRONOUNCING
PROPER NOUNS

PROPER NOUNS

A proper noun is a specific name for a person, place, or thing where the first letter of each word is capitalized. Following are a few examples of proper nouns.

- An example of a girl's first name is **Elizabeth**. An example of a last name is **Smith**. An example of a full name is **Elizabeth Rose Smith**. An example of a nickname is **Liz**.

- An example of a country is **France**. An example of a city is **Paris**.

- Examples of famous places include **Disneyland**, the **Sydney Opera House**, and the **Eiffel Tower**.

- Examples of companies include **Nike**, **Apple**, **Toyota**, **Coca Cola**, and **Amazon**.

Note that proper nouns begin with uppercase letters.

Proper nouns can be challenging to pronounce because many proper nouns don't follow the usual rules for pronouncing English. Following are some examples.

- The **h** in the name **Thomas** is silent. This name begins with the **t** sound (not the **th** sound).

- The word **Wednesday** is pronounced **Wenz–day.**

- **Nike** looks like it should have a single syllable with a silent **e**, but it is actually pronounced as two syllables with a long **e** after the **k.**

- The **Ju** in the name **Juan** makes the **w** sound and the **J** in the name **Jose** makes the **h** sound.

- The country **Qatar** doesn't have a **u** after the **q**, and the **q** makes the **k** sound.

We will explore a variety of common proper nouns which are difficult to pronounce.

TYPES OF PROPER NOUNS

Following are examples of proper nouns:

- A person's name, like **George Washington.**

- A location, like **Los Angeles, California, USA.**

- A geographic feature, like **Mount Everest.**

- Days of the week: **Sunday, Monday, Tuesday, Wednesday, Thursday, Friday,** and **Saturday.**

- Months of the year: **January, February, March, April, May, June, July, August, September, October, November,** and **December.**

- Holidays, like **Valentine's Day** and **Thanksgiving.**

- Book titles, like **The Lord of the Rings.**

- Store names, like **Amazon** and **Whole Foods.**

- Historical events, like **World War II.**

- Buildings, like **Empire State** and **Eiffel Tower.**

GIVEN NAMES

When a name begins with **Th**, sometimes the **h** is silent:

Thomas (t + short o + m + uh + s)

Theresa (t + uh + r + long e + s + uh)

Sometimes **ch** makes the **k** sound:

Chloe (k + l + long o + long e)

Michael (m + long i + k + uh + l)

Occasionally, **ph** makes the **v** sound:

Stephen (s + t + long e + v + uh + n)

An **e** at the end of a name isn't always silent:

Penelope (p + uh + n + short e + l + uh + p + long e)

Phoebe (f + long e + b + long e)

Hermione (h + uh + r + m + long i + uh + n + long e)

Occasionally, **se** makes the **sh** sound:

Sean (sh + aw + n)

175

Sometimes, **j** makes the **h** sound or the **w** sound:

Jose (h + long o + z + long a)

Jaime (h + long i + m + long e)

Juan (w + short o + n)

Joaquin (w + short o + k + long e + n)

A **y** at the beginning of a name can make a vowel sound:

Yvonne (long e + v + short o + n)

Vowel groups don't always sound as you might expect:

Raul (r + short o + long u + l)

Naomi (n + long a + long o + m + long e)

Louise (l + long u + long e + z)

Sometimes, **x** makes the **z** sound or the **sh** sound:

Xavier (z + long a + v + long e + uh + r)

Xiu (sh + long e + short oo)

COUNTRIES

Following are a variety of countries that are difficult to pronounce:

Afghanistan (silent h)

Azerbaijan (ai makes long i)

Belize (b + uh + l + long e + z)

Bhutan (silent h)

Chile (e makes long e)

Colombia (c + uh + l + short u + m + b + long e + uh)

Czech Republic (ch + short e + k)

Djibouti (j + short i + b + long u + t + long e)

Ecuador (cu makes kw)

Egypt (long e + j + short i + p + t)

Fiji (f + long e + j + long e)

Georgia (j + similar to long o + r + j + uh)

Ghana (g + short o + n + uh)

Guatemala (gu makes gw)

Guinea (g + short i + n + long e)

Guyana (g + long i + short a + n + uh)

Haiti (h + long a + t + long e)

Iraq (short i + r + short a + k)

Israel (short i + z + r + long e + uh + l)

Jamaica (j + uh + m + long a + k + uh)

Kazakhstan (silent h)

Kiribati (k + short i + r + uh + b + short a + s)

Kuwait (k + long u + w + long a + t)

Kyrgyzstan (silent z)

Liechtenstein (ie makes short i, ch makes k)

Luxembourg (our makes ir)

Malawi (m + short o + l + short o + w + long e)

Malaysia (si makes zh)

Mali (m + short o + l + long e)

Mauritius (ti makes sh + long e)

Morocco (m + uh + r + short o + k + long o)

Mozambique (que makes k)

Nauru (n + short o + long u + r + long u)

Nicaragua (gu makes gw)

Palau (p + short o + l + ow)

Paraguay (gu makes gw)

Qatar (k + short o + t + short o + r)

Russia (si makes sh)

Rwanda (r + long u + short o + n + d + uh)

Saudi Arabia (au makes ow)

Switzerland (z makes s)

Thailand (silent h)

Uruguay (y + oo + r + uh + g + w + long a)

Venezuela (zu makes zw)

Zimbabwe (ends with long a)

WORLD CITIES

Following are a variety of world cities that are difficult to pronounce:

Shanghai, China (ai makes long i)

Delhi, India (silent h)

Beijing, China (b + long a + j + short i + ng)

Mumbai, India (ai makes long i)

Dhaka, Bangladesh (silent h)

Cairo, Egypt (ai makes long i)

Seoul, South Korea (eou makes long o)

Bangkok, Thailand (not a distinct clear g)

Tehran, Iran (silent h)

Baghdad, Iraq (silent h)

Rio de Janeiro, Brazil (j makes zh)

Melbourne, Australia (ou makes uh)

Kolkata, India (k + aw + l + k + short u + t + uh)

Nairobi, Kenya (ai makes long i)

Buenos Aires, Argentina (bu makes bw)

Kiev, Ukraine (k + long e + short e + f)

Dubai, United Arab Emirates (ai makes long i)

Taipei, Taiwan (t + long i + p + long a)

Bucharest, Romania (ch makes k)

Kathmandu, Nepal (silent h)

Tijuana, Mexico (t + long e + uh + w + short o + n + uh)

Guadalajara, Mexico (gu makes gw, j makes h)

Kyoto, Japan (k + long e + long o + t + long o)

Prague, Czech Republic (silent ue)

Ljubljana, Slovenia (silent j's)

Ottawa, Canada (short o + t + uh + w + uh)

Phnom Penh, Cambodia (p + uh + n + short o + m)

Pyongyang, North Korea (no distinct clear g's)

Reykjavik, Iceland (j makes y)

STATES IN THE USA

Following are a variety of states (in the United States of America) that are difficult to pronounce:

Arkansas (as makes aw)

Connecticut (middle c is silent)

Georgia (j + similar to long o + r + j + uh)

Hawaii (h + uh + w + short o + long e)

Illinois (silent s)

Louisiana (l + long u + long e + z + long e + short a + n + uh)

Missouri (m + short i + z + oo + r + long e)

New Hampshire (ire makes uh + r)

Note that Louisiana has three accepted pronunciations. The alternative pronunciations are:

Louisiana (l + long u + uh + z + long e + short a + n + uh)

Louisiana (l + long u + z + long e + short a + n + uh)

CITIES IN THE USA

Following are a variety of cities (in the United States of America) that are difficult to pronounce:

Phoenix, Arizona (oe makes long e)

San Jose, California (j makes h)

Louisville, Kentucky (l + long u + uh + v + uh + l)

Albuquerque, New Mexico (qu's make k's, not kw's)

Tucson, Arizona (silent c, long u)

Raleigh, North Carolina (r + aw + l + long e)

Minneapolis, Minnesota (e is long, o makes uh)

New Orleans, Louisiana (aw + r + l + long e + uh + n + z)

Wichita, Kansas (w + short i + ch + uh + t + aw)

Anaheim, California (ei makes long i)

Pittsburgh, Pennsylvania (silent h)

Anchorage, Alaska (ch makes k)

Newark, New Jersey (n + long u + uh + r + k)

Lincoln, Nebraska (second l is silent)

Durham, North Carolina (silent h)

Norfolk, Virginia (silent l)

Chesapeake, Virginia (e, a, ea, e vowel pattern)

Hialeah, Florida (h + long i + uh + l + long e + uh)

Boise, Idaho (two syllables, long e)

Baton Rouge, Louisiana (r + long u + zh)

Des Moines, Iowa (two silent s's)

Cheyenne, Wyoming (sh + long i + short a + n)

Juneau, Alaska (j + long u + n + long o)

Pierre, South Dakota (p + short i + r)

Montpelier, Vermont (ier makes y + uh + r)

Sioux Falls, South Dakota (s + long u)

Eugene, Oregon (y + long u + j + long e + n)

Mesquite, Texas (m + short e + s + k + long e + t)

APPENDIX
TECHNICAL
TERMS

TERMINOLOGY

Until now, we have avoided using technical jargon in order to help make the concepts clear to everybody, regardless of their background. If you're reading a spelling or phonics book, but aren't familiar with words like diphthong or Schwa, this new vocabulary can add to the challenge of trying to understand the main ideas. On the other hand, if you learn this vocabulary, this will be helpful if:

- You read a book or online article about spelling or phonics that uses technical terms.

- You work with an instructor or tutor. If you and the instructor both know the terminology, you can communicate more precisely about phonics.

- You discuss ideas with other students who are familiar with the terminology.

digraph: a pair of letters that represents a single sound, like **ph, ou,** or **ck.**

diphthong: a combined vowel sound that begins as one vowel and ends as another vowel. Some common diphthongs include:

- the **au** diphthong: the **ou** in **cloud** or **brown**

- the **oi** diphthong: the **oi** in **noise** or **boy**

- the **ou** diphthong: the long **a** in **rain** or **plane**

- the **ai** diphthong: the long **i** in **right** or **bite**

- the **ei** diphthong: the long **o** in **road** or **no**

Note that **diphthongs** refer to how you make the vowel sound with your mouth (not how you spell the word). Although some diphthongs are spelled with a pair of vowels (like **cloud**), many are not (like **ride**). In comparison, a digraph is pair of letters (like **sh** or **ou**) that make a single sound.

phoneme: a single individual sound, like **f** or **t**.

grapheme: one or more letters that represent a single phoneme, like **b, ch,** or **igh.** For example, the graphemes **f, ph,** and **gh** correspond to the phoneme **f** (since **f, ph,** and **gh** can each make the **f** sound).

blend: separate sounds that are put together, like **ct** or **fr,** where you can still hear the individual phonemes.

r-controlled vowel: a vowel that sounds a little different before an **r.** Compare **shape** with **share**.

onset: the initial consonant sounds of a syllable, like the **cl** in **clap** or the **r** in **rain**.

rime: the vowel sound plus any following consonant sounds of a syllable, like the **ap** in **clap** or the **ou** in **you**. For example, in the word **shown,** the onset is **sh** and the rime is **own**.

Schwa: the soft **uh** sound that is commonly heard in unstressed syllables of multi-syllable words. Examples include the **a** in **ago,** the **e** in **item,** the **i** in **cousin,** the **o** in **carrot,** and the **u** in **circus.** The Schwa sound is represented by the symbol **ə,** which looks like an **e** that is both upside down and backwards.

SYMBOLS

ā, ē, ī, ō, and ū: long vowel sounds.

ä: the short **o** sound, like **hot** and the **a** in **father**.

ô: the **aw** sound, like **saw** and **long**.

oo: the (short) **oo** sound, like **book** and **put**.

o͞o: the long **u** sound, like **moon** and **tune**. It's the same

   as what we have called ū (the long **u**) in this book.

ʉ: the vowel in the **ir** sound, like **sir** and **her**.

ə: the Schwa symbol, like the **a** in **ago**.

ŋ: the **ng** sound that doesn't make a clear distinct **g**, like

   ring and **being**. You also hear it in **pink** before the **k**.

th: the **th** sound like **the** and **that**.

th: the **th** sound like **thin** and **thing**.

ANSWER KEY

Part 1

Page 18

1. dogs, was, music

(the others make **s** sounds)

2. grass, space

(the others make **z** sounds)

Page 22

1. **z** (doors)

2. **s** (star)

3. **z** (music)

4. **sh** (sugar)

5. **s** (miss)

6. **zh** (treasure)

7. **s** (mister)

8. **z** (husband)

Page 23

1. cake, cute, scar

(the others make a soft **c**)

2. nice, icy, cities

(the others make a hard **c**)

3. c̲ircle / ac̲cept / bic̲ycle / conc̲ert

(the **cc** in accept makes the **ks** sound)

Page 24

1. lunch, choose

(dish and especially make a **sh** sound; back makes a **k** sound)

2. chain, pinch

(the others make a **k** sound)

Page 28

1. galaxy, goat, gut

(the others make a **j** sound)

2. danger, region, apology

(the others make a hard **g**)

3. cough, tough

(the other **gh**'s are silent)

4. sight, fight, through

(the others make an **f** sound)

5. **g** (great)

6. **j** (giant)

7. **g** (get)

8. **f** (tough)

Page 30

1. badge, bridges, fudge, changing

(angry makes a hard **g**)

2. danger, soldiers, education

(the others make a hard **g**)

3. hunger, strongest

(the others end with the **ng** sound, which doesn't include a hard **g** at the end, but which is different from just an **n** sound; in hunger and strongest, the first syllable ends with the **ng** sound, while a hard **g** begins the second syllable)

4. fang, sung, doing

(in the others, a hard **g** begins the second syllable)

5. **g** (stronger; it's **ng** + **g**)

6. **j** (stranger)

7. yes (beginning the second syllable)

8. no

Page 33
1. thing (cloth)
2. that (clothe)
3. thing (thieves)
4. that (than)
5. that (though)
6. thing (thumb)
7. thing (thrill)
8. thing (thankful)

Page 36
1. lotion, nutrition, ambitious
   (tiara makes a **t** sound;
   fortune makes a **ch** sound)
2. ritual, century, lecture
   (century often has a **ch** sound,
   but may be pronounced with a
   sh sound; tube makes a **t** sound;
   the first **t** in tuition makes a **t**
   sound and the **ti** in tuition
   makes a **sh** sound)
3. liked, pinched, washed
   (the others make a **d** sound)
4. rained, hired, seated
   (the others make a **t** sound;
   since the **c** in raced makes the **s**
   sound, the **ed** makes a **t** sound)
5. id (since cheat ends with **t**)
6. t (since look ends with **k**)
7. id (since need ends with **d**)
8. d (since change ends with a **j**
   sound)

Page 38
1. r (the **r** in war)
2. w (the **w** in war)
3. r (wrote)
4. w (while)
5. r (rush)
6. w (watch)
7. r (wrench)
8. h (who)

Page 39
1. phone, graph, rough
2. quit, request, question
   (the others make a **k** sound)

Page 40
1. knit, knot

Page 44
1. took, king, block, blink
   (**k** is silent in knot)
2. zone, amazing, xerox (first x)
   (pizza makes a **ts** sound;
   anxious makes a **ksh** sound)
3. azure, seizure
   (pretzel makes a **ts** sound)
4. pizza, pretzel
   (pizza and pretzel make **ts**
   sounds, which includes an **s**
   sound; exam makes a **gz** sound;
   anxiety makes a **gz** sound)
5. fox, taxes, expect
   (the others make **gz** sounds)
6. exact, examine
   (anxious makes a **ksh** sound;
   the others make **ks** sounds)
7. your, young, usually, beyond
   (the **u**'s in usually make **y** + long
   u sounds)

8. one, once

(onion and union include a

consonant **y** sound)

Page 46

1. **w** (wrote)

2. **l** (chalk)

3. **n** (knob)

4. **gh** (straight)

5. **h** (scholar)

6. **t** (wrestle)

7. **b** (lamb)

Page 53

1. pencil, nice

(the others make **z** sounds)

2. prize, desert, fries, xylophone

(picnics make an **s** sound)

3. can, make, unique

(race makes an **s** sound;

the **k** is silent in knot)

4. station, mission, sure

(vision makes a **zh** sound)

5. actual, fortunate

(chef and action make **sh**

sounds; school makes a **k** sound)

6. jar, angel, fudge, apologize

(forgive makes a hard **g**)

7. gear, girl, guess

(gentle makes a **j** sound;

cough makes an **f** sound)

8. off, cough, graph

(of makes a **v** sound;

the **gh** is silent in though)

Page 54

1. what, rewind, sandwich

(whom makes an **h** sound;

write makes an **r** sound)

2. how, who, whole

(why makes a **w** sound;

the **h** is silent in hour)

3. beige, vision, treasure

(the others make **j** sounds)

4. quick, quiet, request

(the others make **k** sounds)

5. breath, without

(the others sound like that)

6. these, bathe

(the others sound like thing)

7. unit, yes

(the **y**'s in eye and today take

part in vowel sounds)

8. k⃞ni⃞ght, thum⃞bs, throu⃞gh,

h⃞onorary, eighty-tw⃞o

Part 2

Page 60

1. pays, stays, played, saying

(says makes the short **e** sound)

2. paid, drain

(said and against make short **e**

sounds; plaid makes the short **a**)

Page 62

1. feel, seen, needle, cheetah

(been makes the short **i** sound)

2. eat, steam, streak

(steak makes the long **a** sound;

thread makes the short **e** sound)

Page 65
1. weird, neither, receive
   (vein makes the long **a** sound;
   foreign makes the short **i** sound)
2. piece, field, relief
   (the others make long **i** sounds)
3. beige, weight, neighbor
   (height makes the long **i** sound;
   ceiling makes the long **e** sound)
4. flies, denies

Page 66
1. law, draw, faucet
   (laughter makes the short **a**
   sound)

Page 67
1. mission, nation, fictional

Page 68
1. boat, goal, foamy, approach
   (abroad makes the **aw** sound)
2. toe, echoes, tomatoes
   (doesn't makes the short **u**;
   horseshoe makes the long **u**)

Page 69
1. join, moisture
   (porpoise and tortoise make soft
   uh sounds; doing makes the
   long **u** + short **i** sounds)
2. boy, annoy, loyal, voyage,
   royalty (all five words)

Page 71
1. wool, wooden, bookcase
   (the others make long **u** sounds)
2. food, booth, mushroom
   (the others make short **oo**
   sounds)
3. bloody, flooding
   (foot makes the short **oo** sound,
   not the short **u** sound)
4. flooring, doorknob
   (poorly makes the short **oo**
   sound)

Page 75
1. soul, dough
   (out and amount make the **ow**
   sound; southern makes the
   short **u** sound)
2. soup, through
3. young, touch, cousin
   (could makes the short **oo**
   sound; youth makes the long **u**)
4. would've, shouldn't
5. jealous, precious
6. about, shout, mouth
   (enough makes the short **u**;
   bought makes the **aw** sound)
7. fought, coughing
   (cloud and mouse make the **ow**
   sound; tough makes the short **u**)
8. tournament, courageous
   (pour makes the **aw** sound like
   storm, though you might hear
   it more like a long **o**; sour and
   flour make the **ow** sound)

Page 76
1. growth, showed
   (the others make the **ow** sound)

Page 77
1. glued, rescue, avenue
   (guest makes the short **e** sound;
   the **ue** is silent in league)

Page 78
1. juicy, bruise, pursuit
   (suite makes the long **e** sound;
   disguise makes the long **i** sound)
2. built, circuit, biscuit
   (the others make the long **u**)

Page 81
1. eighty, sleigh, straighten
   (caught makes the **aw** sound;
   heighten makes the long **i**)
2. light, tonight
   (the others make the long **a**)
3. dough, though
   (fought makes the **aw** sound;
   through makes the long **u**;
   roughly makes the short **u**)
4. through
   (ought, cough, and bought make
   the **aw** sound; though makes
   the long **o** sound)
5. tough, enough
   (the others make the **aw** sound)
6. naughty, thought, daughter
   (rough makes the short **u**;
   though makes the long **o** sound)
7. drought
8. tough, enough
   (**gh** is silent in the other words)

Page 84
1. made, tale, crazy
2. eve, extreme, evening
3. ice, shiny, dining
4. joke, pony, clothing
5. duty, assume

Page 87
1. cane, danger, making
2. and, man
   (woman makes the soft **uh**)
3. all, ball, chalk
   (was makes the short **u** sound;
   vocal makes the soft **uh** sound)
4. calm, swap, father
   (any makes the short **e** sound;
   call makes the **aw** sound, which
   is slightly different from the
   short **o** sound – call makes a
   vowel sound like saw, whereas
   calm makes a vowel like hot)
5. wasn't
   (the others make the short **a**)
6. alone, final, lovable, summary
   (the **a** in scary makes the short
   e sound like the **ea** in bear)
7. many, anybody
   (zany makes the long **a**; the
   others make the short **a**)

Page 90
1. he, delete, beware

   (the first two **e**'s in delete are both long)
2. we, we've, preview, concrete
3. them, spent

   (pretty makes the short **i** sound)
4. sled, dressed

   (acted and folded make the **id** sound)
5. valet, gourmet
6. panel, staple, absent, celebrate
7. women, prettiest
8. handed, seated, greeted

Page 92
1. wild, tiger, dining
2. tin, children

   (spaghetti makes the long **e**)
3. taxicab, pepperoni
4. notify, holiday, politics, terrible

Page 96
1. told, cozy, hoping
2. hot, shock

   (today makes the soft **uh** sound)
3. gone, strong, belong

   (gone can also make the short **o**)
4. undo, proven, hairdo
5. done, shovel, sponge
6. police, reason, decorate, originate
7. women
8. wolf, wolves

Page 100
1. duty, lunatic, parachute
2. tutor, junior, ruling
3. bus, unlike

   (busy makes the short **i**)
4. mule, united, excuse, humorous
5. bonus, circus, spatula, century
6. burial, buried
7. busily, business
8. bush, pudding

Page 102
1. copy, country
2. defy, hyper
3. analysis

Page 109
1. her, worse, nurse
2. actor, dollar, father
3. hair, pear, share
4. hard, heart

   (war sounds a little different from car, just like warm sounds a little different from farm)
5. born, warm, sword, forth
6. near, pier, cheer
7. pure, sure

   (the others make the **ir** sound like sir)
8. tire, choir, admire, acquire

Page 112
1. **e** (forgive)
2. **i** (bruise)
3. **o** (tough)
4. **a** (stealthy)
5. **o** (leopard)
6. **i** (juicy)
7. **ue** (league)

Page 114
1. great, train, survey
2. razor, weight, ballet
3. camp, plaid
   (many makes the short **e** sound; the others make the long **a**)
4. laugh, chance
   (was makes the short **u** sound; want makes the short **o** sound; chalk makes the **aw** sound)
5. seen, before, monkey
   (an alternate pronunciation for before is with a short **i** sound)
6. ski, penny, receipt
7. gentle, guess
8. said, buried, leopard
   (both vowels in women make the short **i** sound; people makes the long **e** and the soft **uh** sounds)

Page 115
1. eye, virus, price
2. denied, supply, flight
3. hint, myth
4. busy, built, women, mystery
   (bury makes the short **e** sound)
5. most, grow, float
6. rosy, cargo, boulder
7. knot, father
   (son and brother make the short **u** sound; who makes the long **u**)
8. got, taco, honest
   (the **a** in taco makes the short **o**, whereas the **o** in taco makes the long **o**; done makes the short **u** sound; stone makes the long **o**)

Page 116
1. who, crew, soon
   (sew makes the long **o** sound)
2. clue, juice, through
   (book makes the short **oo** sound)
3. done, under, bloody, double
4. walk, strong, caught, brought
5. again, double, visitor, support
6. push, look, good, should
   (tooth makes the long **u** sound)
7. toy, enjoy, spoil, noisy
   (choir makes the **w** + long **i** sound)
8. mouth, eyebrow

Part 3

Page 121

1. out-side (2)
   grad-ed (2)
   spoiled (1)
   brought (1)
   in-ter-sect (3)
   lan-guage (2)
   ga-rage (2)
   spa-ghet-ti (3)
   eye-sight (2)
   un-der-stand-ing (4)
   count-er-top (3)
   in-vis-i-bil-i-ty (6)
2. rea-son (2)
   re-use (2)
   re-ac-tion (3)
   ar-e-a (3)
   flea (1)
   heav-y (2)
   be-ing (2)
   eight (1)
   weigh-ing (2)
   an-cient (2)
   sci-ence (2)
   hap-pi-est (3)
3. per-sua-sive (3)
   vi-o-lent (3)
   e-mo-tio-nal (4)
   re-o-pen (3)
   leop-ard (2)
   le-o-tard (3)
   co-op-er-ate (4)
   i-nit-ial (3) (i-nish-uhl)
   i-nit-i-a-tion (5)
   cou-ra-geous (3)
   un-u-su-al (4) (un-yu-zhuh-wuhl)
   e-speci-al-ly (4)
   Note: In print, we would
   hyphenate es-pe-cial-ly, but in
   speech, we say e-spesh-uhl-ly.

Page 127

1. man / mess / sic / cept / tan
2. ca / fu / po + lo / go / ri
3. wil + dered / per + nal / an /
   ver + sion
   (personal = per-suh-nal)
4. pa / de / di / va
   (dilated = di-lat-id)
5. hope / life + time / mate / vise /
   use
   (the first two **e**'s in televise
   aren't silent)
6. ple / kle / dle / tle / tle
7. joy / rai / count / laugh / shoul
8. car / lar / gour / ler / har + der

Note the distinction between syllables
in written hyphenation and syllables
in pronunciation. For example, in
print, we would hyphenate "rising" as
ris-ing, whereas in pronunciation, we
say ri-sing. In this set of exercises, we
are concerned with the pronunciation
key (ri-sing is correct for this), not
written hyphenation (so ris-ing is
incorrect for our purposes).

Page 139

1. in / pre / un
   re / de / in
   inter / con / ex
   intro / under / im
2. er / ing / ment
   ful / ly / ize
   ify / able / ous
   itioner (i + tion + er) / ingly
   (ing + ly) / ize
3. fens / wild / sist
   rot / gram / meas
   tract / tend / vers
   vis / worth / cite
   port / creat / stood

Page 141
1. for + ever
2. down + stairs
3. book + case
4. up + beat
5. your + self
6. there + fore
7. any + one
8. further + more

Page 146
1. fa / range / pur
   heav / dol / tend
   ny / qui / plan
   den / fun / lect
2. grum / plain / wal
   round / ac / per
   mo / hon / pare
   car / chine / bove
   (carry, machine, and above are
   exceptions to the usual rules:
   nouns and adjectives usually
   place stress on the first syllable,
   and verbs tend to place stress on
   the second syllable)
3. lis / fer / men
   tel / fas / gin
   planned / shel / curred
   spelled / fas / hap

Page 159
1. around / open / bonus
   fasten / peril / nervous
   (the **t** is silent in fasten)
   agent / offense / passion
   (offense usually begins with **uh**,
   except in the context of sports)
   proper / parade / mention
2. animal / uniform / opposite
   relative / allowance / injury
   appearance / excellent /
       transition

(transition = tran-zish-uhn)
holiday / history / technical
3. elevator / apology /
       disagreement
   occasional / education /
       arithmetic
   (education can alternatively be
   pronounced with a soft **uh** in the
   second and last syllables)
   application / informative /
       biology
   opportunity / harmoniously /
       counterproductive

Page 160
1. bottom / cactus / surround
   martial / avoid / comfort
   listen / suggest / shuffle
   (the **t** is silent in listen)
   collect / nature / wasn't
2. practical / visitor / century
   terrible / verify / elephant
   hesitant / usual / resistance
   origin / avenue / production
3. analysis / intelligence /
       especially
   certificate / originate /
       invisible
   suspiciously / appreciate /
       refrigerate
   astronomical / determination
       miscellaneous

INDEX

A

a (long) **56**, 60-63, 66, 79, 83-86, 89

a (making aw sound) 85

a (making short e) 86

a (making short o) 85

a (making short u) 86

a (making uh) 85, 86, 149, 151, 152

a (short) **57**, 60, 66, 80, 83-86

a (silent) 111

a (sound) 85-87

a_e 59, **83-84**, 85

aa 82

ab 130, 136

able 86, 132, 136, 154

ae 82

ai 60

aigh 79

ain 153

al 86, 132, 136, 154

ance 156

ange 86

ant 157

anti 130

ao 82

ar 152

ary 152

aste 86

ate 133, 155

au 66, 79-80

augh 79-80

aw (sound) 57, 66, 68, 73-75, 79, 80, 85, 93, 95, 106

aw + r 71

ay 60

B

b (silent) 45

b (sound) 16

bi 131

blend 188

C

c (hard) 17, **23**

c (silent) 45

c (soft) 17, **23**

cc (making k sound) 23

ce (making sh sound) 24

ch (sound) 24, 34

ci (making sh sound) 24

cial 156

J

K

L

tract 136

tri 131

tu (making ch sound) 34

U

u (long) **56**, 66, 68, 70, 72-75, 77, 78, 80, 83, 93

u (making oo sound) 97

u (making short e) 98

u (making short i) 98

u (making uh) 98, 150, 151

u (making w sound) 26, 39

u (short) **57**, 66, 68, 70, 73-75, 80, 83 86, 93, 97-98

u (silent) 77, 111

u (sound) 97-100

u (with y sound) 43, 66, 77, 97, 108

u_e 59, **83-84**, 97

ue 77

uh 58, 67, 69, 73-75, 85-86, 88-89, 91, 94-95, 98, 102, 107, **147-160**, 189

ui 78

un 98, 129, 130, 137

under 131

uni 131

unstressed syllable 147-160

uoy 82

ur 104

ury 153

US cities 183-184

US states 182

uu 82

uy 82

V

v (sound) 16

vers 134, 136

vis 134

voc 134, 136

vowel + r sounds 103-109

vowel + r syllables 123

vowel sounds (summary) 6-10

vowel team syllables 123

vowels, long 56

vowels, short 57-58

vowels (silent) 111

AUDIO BOOK

The Art of Phonics will be available in audio book format in the summer of 2018. Listen along to the audio book to hear each word pronounced as you read it.

THE ART OF SPELLING

Spelling and phonics go hand-in-hand together:

- In *The Art of Spelling*, you learn techniques for how to spell a word after you've heard it spoken.

- In *The Art of Phonics*, you learn techniques for how to pronounce a word that you see in writing.

The Art of **PHONICS**	
tough	through
though	thorough
thought	throughout
Jenny Pearson	

The Art of **SPELLING**		
s	spag	spaghet
sp	spagh	spaghett
spa	spaghe	spaghetti
Jenny Pearson		

CURSIVE HANDWRITING

It's never too late to learn cursive handwriting.

- Learn how to write the cursive alphabet.

- Practice writing words, phrases, and sentences.

- Challenge yourself to remember how to write each letter in cursive.

- Writing prompts offer additional practice.

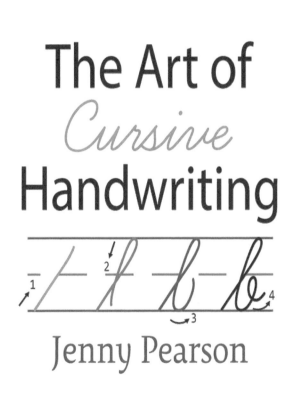

COLORING BOOKS

Coloring books aren't just for kids. They are popular among teens and adults, too. Coloring provides a relaxing way to take your mind off of stress, and lets you use your creativity.

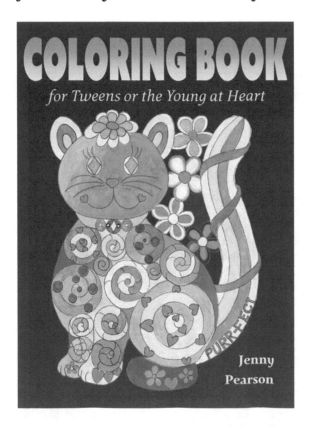

20428357R00120